A MOTHER'S HEART

JEAN FLEMING

NAVPRESS

BRINGING TRUTH TO LIFE
NavPress Publishing Group
P.O. Box 35001, Colorado Springs, Colorado 80935

OUR GUARANTEE TO YOU

We believe so strongly in the message of our books that
we are making this quality guarantee to you. If for any
reason you are disappointed with the content of this
book, return the title page to us with your name and
address and we will refund to you the list price of the
book. To help us serve you better, please briefly describe
why you were disappointed. Mail your refund request to:
NavPress, P.O. Box 35002, Colorado Springs, CO 80935.

The Navigators is an international Christian organization. Our mission is to reach, disciple, and equip
people to know Christ and to make Him known through successive generations. We envision multitudes
of diverse people in the United States and every other nation who have a passionate love for Christ, live
a lifestyle of sharing Christ's love, and multiply spiritual laborers among those without Christ.

NavPress is the publishing ministry of The Navigators. NavPress publications help believers learn
biblical truth and apply what they learn to their lives and ministries. Our mission is to stimulate spiritual
formation among our readers.

Library of Congress Catalog Card Number: 95-26710
ISBN 08910-99441

Cover photograph: Michael Goldman/FPG International

Unless otherwise identified, all Scripture quotations in this publication are taken from the *HOLY
BIBLE: NEW INTERNATIONAL VERSION®* (NIV®). Copyright © 1973, 1978, 1984 by International
Bible Society. Used by permission of Zondervan Publishing House. All rights reserved. Other versions
used include: *The Living Bible* (TLB), © 1971 owned by assignment by the Illinois Regional Bank N.A.
(as trustee), used by permission of Tyndale House Publishers, Inc., Wheaton, IL 60189; *The New
English Bible* (NEB), © 1961, 1970, The Delegates of the Oxford University Press and The Syndics of the
Cambridge University Press; and the *King James Version* (KJV).

Fleming, Jean.
        A mother's heart / Jean Fleming.—[Rev. ed.]
        p.   cm.
        ISBN 0-89109-944-1
        1. Mothers—Religious life. 2. Child rearing—Religious aspects—
        Christianity. I. Title.
        BV4847.F46 1996
        248.8'431—dc20   95-26710
                                                                                   CIP

Printed in the United States of America

    6 7 8 9 10 11 12 13 14 15/05 04 03 02 01

FOR A FREE CATALOG OF
NAVPRESS BOOKS & BIBLE STUDIES,
CALL 1-800-366-7788 (USA)
or 1-416-499-4615 (CANADA)

CONTENTS

For my husband, Roger,
and my children, Matthew, Beth, and Graham,
who made me what I am today—a mother,
and for Anna E. Myers, my mother

FOREWORD

I first met Jean Fleming at a conference here in the United States as she and her family were en route from one strenuous missionary assignment in Korea to another in Japan. Her toddler, Matthew, clung to her skirt while baby Beth rested in her arms. People pressed around wanting to talk with this dear missionary friend who had been away so long and would soon leave again.

Although Jean graciously spoke with each friend, her children obviously did not feel excluded or rejected. Rather, they were the focus of Jean's concern, and the friends were being warmly drawn into Jean's family circle.

A few years later, Jean and Roger returned from their overseas assignment and lived near us for a time. Another son, Graham, had joined their family. I saw Jean often and observed the ongoing training of her children. Jean taught me the importance of giving extended time to review each child's strengths and needs, and then to make a plan to develop the strengths and meet the needs. I observed as she encouraged her children and stimulated them to develop physically, artistically, and socially.

Jean's mothering strengths are enhanced as she injects humor, fun, and surprise into family living. The Fleming home is a fun and happy place.

Jean and Roger not only plan creatively for their children, but also pray consistently for them and for themselves as parents. They take their family seriously as a trust from God.

From her own rich experience of dedicated parenting and from research and observation of others, Jean offers a fine balance of motivation and practical suggestions for parents who truly care about the development of their children. She calls parents to commitment in their task. I would have benefited greatly if we had had this book in our early years as parents, and I know you will want to refer to it again and again for help, ideas, and encouragement.

Mary A. White
1982

PREFACE

Advice on child rearing is often confusing, sometimes humorous, and occasionally irrational, but it is always interesting.

It is usually best to have a nap right after lunch. After lunch simply say, in a breezy, cheerful, self-confident, firm but not harsh, assured but not domineering, soft but audible tone, "It is time to have our NAPPIE now." If you have done this properly, most children, not all children, will usually, not always, sometimes, go to bed without protesting. (From *How to Raise Children at Home in Your Spare Time,* Stein and Day, 1966)

Beat a child every day; if you don't know what he's done to deserve the beating, he will. (An old folk saying)

Go directly—see what she is doing and tell her she mustn't. (From an 1872 cartoon in *Punch,* as quoted in *The Royal Bank of Canada Monthly Letter*)

All this is little help to mothers who already feel baffled by their parenting assignment. We long for helpful input to crystallize our thinking, and practical suggestions on how to provide better training within our families.

Even God—the perfect Parent—has rebellious, unpredictable children. "I reared children and brought them up," God says in Isaiah 1:2, "but they have rebelled against me."

Reflecting on this, I realized that although parents have a God-given responsibility for bringing up their children, parents cannot bear the total responsibility for how each child turns out. Rather, our goal as parents is to help our children become mature, because our children must ultimately decide for themselves the direction they will take in life.

Acquiring highly developed parenting skills will not ensure that our children will always make choices that are pleasing to God or to us, either now or in the future.

In this book I want to discuss some principles I see in Scripture, to share some thoughts on teaching, and to illustrate these truths with personal examples. As you read my illustrations and suggestions, remember that they are not for your exact imitation, but to stimulate you.

No two families will operate the same, nor should they. Each family's lifestyle should reflect the convictions, values, and personalities of the parents. The principles in Scripture are the same for all of us, but the everyday outworking and application of these principles will differ.

So as you consider the principles and practical suggestions discussed here, think about them, discuss them with your husband, and, most importantly, ask God how He wants you to make these principles and ideas a part of your family's life.

I have addressed this book to mothers as a personal book from the heart of one who is still learning and struggling. But by singling out mothers I do not mean to infer that we have the sole responsibility or even the more significant role in parenting. An equally strong case can be made for the critical contribution of the father.

Roger, my husband, appears frequently in these pages because his loving leadership vitally affects our family. So fathers are most welcome to read this book—but my heart beats for mothers.

In Malachi 4:6, the Lord referred to the future ministry of John the Baptist when He said, "He will turn the hearts of the fathers to their children, and the hearts of the children to their fathers."

My prayer for this book is that God will use it to turn the hearts of mothers to their children.

Jean Fleming
1982

PREFACE FOR THE REVISED EDITION

Fifteen years after I wrote this book, I stand and look back over my shoulder to the past: to my own childhood and to my years as a mother. Then, I turn and see the future materializing before me. From this place at the top of the hill, I see my own children grown and grandchildren racking up one birthday after another until they will, one day, have children of their own.

I look back and acknowledge that times change. (My mother tells me that she put me outside for my naps as a baby, even in cold weather, and that I was potty trained at six months.) To some readers this book may already seem hopelessly outdated. All I know is that, at this point, fifteen years later, as I reviewed the book, I found that I could still sign my name to everything I had written.

I have added a chapter (13), updated the book here and there, deleted, inserted, rewritten, and added questions at the end of each chapter to stimulate personal reflection or discussion with others. Despite the changes, the book remains much the same in spirit and content.

I humbly pass this book on to the next generation of

mothers who must find their own way just as past generations did. Mothering is a creative art, which must be shaped by each woman. At the same time, motherhood isn't an art developed or executed in a vacuum. Each generation of mothers models and, to some extent, defines the calling and task for those who follow. Each mother speaks to the next wave of mothers. Every mother leaves a legacy to future generations.

My prayer is that this book might help women today fill the word *motherhood* with rich meaning. I make no promises, guarantee no plan, and provide no surefire techniques. What I share comes from my own ideals, failures, sincere efforts, and firm conclusions that unless God builds the house, I labor in vain.

This book is a "legacy," something I pass to the next generation. The Latin root of the word legacy is to delegate, to commission, to entrust or command. I hand the torch to mothers entrusted with the future generations with the confidence that just as God has made Himself available to guide mothers throughout history, this generation of mothers will find His help more than sufficient.

Jean Fleming
1995

Chapter One

A CALL TO MOTHERS

The bell rings. The morning session of preschool ends. A five-year-old boy finds his way alone to an empty apartment. He fixes lunch—cookies and corn chips— turns on the television, and watches an afternoon of soap operas until his mother returns from work at five-thirty.

❖   ❖   ❖

A young, well-dressed couple stands beside their barely conscious four-year-old son in the emergency room. The parents tell the doctors he fell into the fireplace. Actually, they wrapped newspapers around his arms and set him on fire.

❖   ❖   ❖

A pale, thin, teenage girl nervously twists a nearly shredded tissue around her finger again and again. She waits numbly to see the doctor. At age fourteen, she is going to have an abortion.

❖   ❖   ❖

A bouncy eleven-year-old pauses outside her parents' bedroom door to rearrange an armload of books, and overhears her mother's voice. "I'm not staying. I'm tired of you and the kids running my life. I want out. You can have the kids if you want them, or you can send them to your mother's or find somebody else to keep them."

Since he was eight he has been on his own. He lived where his parents did, but essentially he was forsaken. He set his own hours, fixed his meals, and did his laundry.

Now at seventeen, he brings home a sixteen-year-old girlfriend. His mother points to a bedroom door and says, "She can stay in there, and you stay in your room."

Eyeing his mother fiercely, he counters, "Where were you when I needed you? She stays in my room."

Mothers, all is not well. Sadly, each of the above incidents actually happened, and incidents like them occur daily. Although we may be able to do little to alter the outcomes in other families, we are wise to allow these tragic accounts to prod us to examine our own attitudes and actions as mothers.

The underlying attitudes that spawn parental neglect and child abuse may have crept quietly into your parenting as well—without your recognizing it. You may never abuse your children, or turn them out on the street, or fail to feed and clothe them; but the viewpoint of the modern generation may have left its marks on your mothering: self-centeredness, lack of commitment, frequent parental absence, or preoccupation with your own interests and concerns.

Is all well in your home?

MOTHERS CARE

As I write this, I feel confident of one thing: almost without exception, *all* mothers want to be good mothers to their children. The very fact that you are reading this book convinces me that you fall into that category. But parenting in an increasingly complex world isn't a simple or easy task, especially for the mother who knows the relationship between mother and child involves more than feeding, clothing, and sheltering her charges.

If you are a mother, you have a calling from God. God entrusts into your care a life, a future, a piece of what the world will become. You become part of the solution or part of the problem that faces us today.

A NEEDY SOCIETY

Politicians, psychologists, educators, law enforcement officers, and medical professionals join religious leaders in expressing their concern for the family. Everyone expects current problems to multiply as troubled youths begin families of their own. Whether our uncaring attitude is revealed by a deliberate act of violence or inadvertent neglect, we are failing to give our children what they desperately need.

THERE'S NO PLACE LIKE HOME

Although some experts predict a future need for more institutional solutions, new studies conclude that "there's no place like home" when it comes to meeting children's needs. Even the Children's Defense Fund organization, involved in out-of-home care for children, began one of its annual reports by confirming the importance of the family.

17

Almost everyone agrees that families are vital to the healthy development of children. Professionals and researchers confirm the conventional wisdom—children need to feel wanted and accepted; they need continuity in their relationships with biological or psychological parents; they need guidance to cope with the demands of growing up; and they need to have some sense that there is a regular, dependable quality to the world.[1]

How interesting that convictions about the importance of the mother's contribution should surface when more and more mothers are spending less and less time with their children.

Is the mother's presence especially important at certain periods in a child's development? Dr. Jack Raskins, psychiatrist at the Children's Orthopedic Hospital and the University of Washington in Seattle, considers the early months most crucial. The key, he says,

is the child's close, unbroken attachment in the early months to the people who care for him. Too much disruption of this imbeds in the personality traits that can be disruptive for a lifetime. People are hyped up over adolescent drug abuse, pregnancies, suicide, and the cults children join. But the same roots underlie them all. The roots are depression and emotional deprivation. These are laid down in the personality in the early months of life. They grow out of poor attachments and inadequate affection and contact for the child in the first months. Attachment to the people who love him and who respond to his needs is nothing less than the foundation of the child's personality.[2]

Is Mom Home?

Financial demands, boredom with the homemaking role, and pressure from the women's movement have moved increasing numbers of mothers into the work place. Each year, more mothers opt to enter the work force while placing their preschool children in the care of others.

Dr. Mary Salter Ainsworth comments,

> Among the most significant developments of psychiatry during the past quarter of a century has been the steady growth of evidence that the quality of the parental care which a child receives in his earliest years is of vital importance for his future mental health.[3]

A mother's presence throughout infancy and the entire preschool stage is important because more learning takes place in the child's first five years than in any comparable period of life. Experts agree that as much as eighty-five percent of a child's character is developed by age five, and the way a child is raised in the early years accounts for at least twenty points of his IQ.

What about the elementary years? Less attention is being given to the mother's influence on this age group, but must we wait for future studies by experts to convince us of our children's need during this period also? In the school-age years peers and teachers add their influences, but the present and engaged mother can interpret, model, reinforce, counter, and moderate the influence of others.

Although our presence can make a difference all through our children's teenage years, a recent study by Junior Achievement reports that parents have lost their place of prominence as the primary influence in their teenagers' lives. In 1960 teenagers ranked their parents first, but today their peers enjoy the place of greatest influence.[4] Friends, television, and music all increasingly influence today's teens.

Have we abdicated? Have we chosen, consciously or unconsciously, to heed another call, to give our energies for some other cause?

DEFINING THE TASK

God established the family as the best possible environment for human development. In God's plan, the family provides a secure and loving framework in which to nourish the child—emotionally, intellectually, physically, and spiritually. The family is called to provide nurture, instruction, and discipline.

From the family the child gains his first understanding of who he is and how he fits into the world around him. He can also acquire a concept of who God is, and how to relate his life to God and His purposes. The child develops values, forms dreams, molds convictions, and sets goals within the family setting. He learns how to make sound judgments and decisions, and how to view life critically. Within his family he forms his view of what it means to be a loving, committed marriage partner and a caring, responsible parent. When parents fail to address these needs, the loss is felt in their children's lives and in society as well.

Mothering has never been an easy or simple task. Every generation of mothers faces a unique set of challenges. Women have reared their children in war-torn lands, in plague-ridden villages, in famine-swollen refugee camps, and in covered wagons facing danger and hardship. The complexities and difficulties we confront are different. But like them, we must define the contribution we will make to the children given to our charge.

A few years ago I met a young woman who told me that after the birth of her second child she decided to quit her public relations job and stay home with her children. She said her intentions were good, but she couldn't figure what to do to fill her days at home. She began to feel that being an "at-home mom" was too small a job for an intelligent, capable woman. Then, someone encouraged her to read *A Mother's Heart*. The book made her aware of areas of contribution to her children's lives she had not previously considered. "Now," she said, "I'm not sure I'm woman enough for the job."

THE ALL-THERE MOTHER

You can be physically present and still not make a positive contribution to your children. You can be there, but not be *all* there. Your mind can be a million miles away, your energy and your ambitions drained by other pursuits. You can focus your attention on your "do list," the television, a good book, or decorating your home, and be oblivious to your child's needs. You may be too busy or too preoccupied to make a significant difference.

Jesus expounds the difference between a good shepherd and a hired hand in John 10. The good shepherd cares deeply about his sheep. He willingly lays down his life for them. The sheep are his, and he loves them.

But the hired hand has a different attitude. The sheep aren't his. Caring for them is only his job. And when a wolf threatens the sheep, the hired hand abandons them. He runs away because he has a shallow concern for the sheep.

We can emulate either the good shepherd or the

21

hired hand in the quality of our commitment to our children.

If we are good shepherds, we will diligently attend to their welfare. Tenderly and wholeheartedly, we will seek their best regardless of the cost to us.

Naturally, we can't expect the daycare worker, the baby-sitter, or the preschool teacher to shepherd our children as lovingly as we can, because the children aren't theirs. God holds us accountable for the children He has placed in our care.

A CALL TO MOTHERS

Webster defines "call" as "a divine vocation or strong inner prompting to a particular course of action."

In every generation mothers must answer the call to *be* what no one else can *be* and to *do* what no one else can *do* for their children. It isn't that mothers can't do many other things, but if they refuse to accept their calling as *mother* some child ends up shortchanged. And the empty space that mother leaves echos for generations.

Mothers are neither the cause of all society's ills nor the saviors of the nation. But the future of society does depend, in part, on what we do with the children under our care. What calling could be more significant or more glorifying to God?

God calls us to bring to our mothering a high level of commitment, and a right perspective born out of a clear vision and a biblical value system. Will you answer His call?

QUESTIONS FOR REFLECTION OR DISCUSSION

1. As you consider your calling as mother, how do you define your job description?

2. You do not mother in a war-torn land or from a covered wagon, but you nonetheless face specific difficulties. As a mother, what challenges do you face?
3. What qualities do an "all-there" mother and a "good shepherd" have in common?
4. In light of your reflections, what one decision might you make to be more the mother you want to be?

NOTES
  1. As quoted by Roger Wilkins, in "An Indictment of Child Care," *The New York Times,* 9 March 1979, p. A-13.
  2. As quoted by Dale Douglas Mills, in "To Work or Not to Work After the Baby Comes," *The Seattle Times Magazine,* 1 July 1979, p. 8.
  3. Mary Salter Ainsworth and John Bowlby, "Deprivation of Maternal Care: A Reassessment of Its Effects," *WHO Public Health Papers,* number 14 (Columbia University Press), p. 13.
  4. Based on a study of growth strategies for Junior Achievement, August 1979–March 1980, p. 8.

Chapter Two

A VISION FOR THE TASK

Is life passing you by while you shampoo the peanut butter out of Junior's hair, then change the baby's diaper again? Does your mothering seem uninteresting, insignificant, even slightly demeaning? Do you feel that your talents and gifts are lying dormant and that your degrees are wasted? Do you feel as though you are in a holding pattern, waiting for your children to leave home or to start school, so you can resume real life?

Feelings of frustration are not unique to mothers. People in any task or profession may feel under-challenged, over-challenged, unappreciated, bored, or misplaced in their occupation. But God wants to lift our eyes above our daily situation and give us a new vision for the assignment He has given us.

Our world desperately needs mothers with such a vision, yet voices are always calling the modern mother in conflicting directions, telling her she needs something more to be liberated and fulfilled.

Not surprisingly, some mothers experience confusion regarding their identity, role, and mission in life.

Perhaps you too are grappling with questions like these: What's really important? What should I give my life to? Will I someday regret what I'm doing now?

WOMAN OF INFLUENCE

Inscribed on a missionary's gravestone are these words: "If I had a thousand lives to give, Korea should have them all." This woman had more dreams and a greater vision for Korea than one lifetime could accomplish. I don't know her name, but her words move me deeply. Korea would have her first life and her thousandth. Her life was poured out for others on foreign soil, yet she had no regrets. She only wished she could do it again and again. But, like all of us, she had only one life to give.

I feel the same way about being a mother. While many women feel the pressure to do something more, I say that if I had another life to give, I'd be a full-time wife and mother again.

I enjoy the breadth of the challenge. The task of mothering can be as broad as I make it. Consider the endless variety of jobs a mother may do: teacher, nurse, dietitian, psychologist, chauffeur, trainer, disciplinarian, seamstress, baseball coach, interior decorator.

This morning, as I raised my eyes from the breakfast dishes, I recognized a neighbor lady coming down our street pushing a paper-cart. As she hand-carried the newspaper to our front porch, I stepped outside and we talked briefly. Her son (our regular paper boy) had won a contest and was enjoying himself in Canada, so she and her younger son were delivering his papers.

"I never thought I'd grow up to be a paper boy," she mused as she left. Mothers can grow up to be many things.

The aspect of mothering that excites me most is knowing I am making a permanent difference in my children's lives. I am a woman of influence. I impart values, stimulate creativity, develop compassion, modify weaknesses, and nurture strengths. I can open life up to another individual. And I can open an individual up to life.

When I read my child a story I am doing far more than entertaining him. I am expanding his world with language, words, thoughts, and imagination.

When I sit beside my child's bed at night to talk and pray, I'm doing far more than cultivating a bedtime ritual. I'm tuning in to what he is thinking, catching up on his day, listening for fears, hopes, and questions. This personal time gives me an opportunity to point him to the Lord Jesus Christ and His relevance to the situations my child faces.

Last night we had a conflict at bedtime. Two of the children had rumbled and grumbled in the bathroom. Each felt unfairly treated and misunderstood by the other. The three of us flopped on my bed to talk. Roger, my husband, had been gone for two weeks of a three-week trip. I felt desperately in need of special help from God. I needed wisdom not only to help the children work through the conflict at hand, but also to give them a deeper understanding of what produces harmony in a home.

As we sat on the bed, I prayed aloud for God's wisdom to deal with the tension between the children. First Peter 4:8 came to mind—"Above all, love each other deeply, because love covers over a multitude of sins." We discussed how God's love covers a multitude of our sins, and how our love for others can help us overlook their faults and enable us to live together harmoniously.

I shared an incident that has profoundly affected our marriage. After the Caesarean delivery of Beth,

Roger sat by my hospital bed watching my sedated sleep. As he waited, he was reading in Ezekiel. His heart missed a beat as he read, " 'Son of man, with one blow I am about to take away from you the delight of your eyes.' . . . So I spoke to the people in the morning, and in the evening my wife died" (Ezekiel 24:16,18).

Roger prayed, "Lord, is Jean going to die?" Overcome with love, he thought of the petty irritations he had occasionally entertained during our marriage. They now seemed so small and meaningless compared to the great love he felt. He resolved that little things would not rob us of a great love. His resolve later became my resolve also.

Neither of us is perfect—but we don't have to be. Our love for each other overlooks a lot. We focus on loving each other, not pointing out each other's weaknesses. "A man's wisdom gives him patience; it is to his glory to overlook an offense" (Proverbs 19:11).

I shared these thoughts with my children in an attempt to motivate them to solve their conflict last night. I cannot measure what influence that single discussion (or others like it) will have. By faith I trust that God will use His Word and these experiences to make a lasting impact on their lives.

Last week a headline in the *Seattle Times* caught my attention: "Busy Little Hands Caught in the Act at Downtown Store." The article reported details of how a mother taught her two-year-old to shoplift. The child stole a matching set of underwear and tucked it into a shopping bag before meeting his mother. (No one could deny that this mother was influencing her child, but she was obviously a negative influence and model.)

Hannah Jowett, the wife of a tailor and draper in Yorkshire, England, was a woman of influence too. Her life and teaching permanently stamped their mark on her son, John Henry Jowett, whose ministry for Christ as a preacher touched people worldwide. His biographer, Arthur Porritt, wrote:

> Jowett went through life chanting the praises of his mother. To the end of her life she was the object of his solicitous care. He never wearied of acknowledging the immensity of his indebtedness to her. "At my mother's knee," he said once, "I gained my sweetest inspirations." To a friend who once asked him whence came his gift for felicitous illustration he replied, "From my mother! It was she who taught me to see—she taught me to see things, and the things within things."[1]

Mothers, God also wants to use your ministry to your children to influence the world for Christ.

INFLUENCING THE WORLD

If we are to develop a godly vision as mothers, we must relate our lives to God and His purposes. We must recognize that God has a purpose for the family. The Christian family is not an island. It is not intended to be an end in itself, but rather a means to a greater end. God wants the Christian family involved in His purpose and plan.

The history of mankind can be stated in capsule form as creation, rebellion, redemption. God created man for His glory, but man rebelled (starting with Adam and continuing to the present). But it is God's plan to redeem His lost creation. God in Christ became a man, was born into a human family, died on the cross for our sins, rose from the dead, and will come again.

29

Before Jesus returned to heaven, He gave His followers this challenging assignment:

> "All authority in heaven and on earth has been given to me. Therefore go and make disciples of all nations, baptizing them in the name of the Father and of the Son and of the Holy Spirit, and teaching them to obey everything I have commanded you. And surely I am with you always, to the very end of the age." (Matthew 28:18-20)

The mission Christ left us is not optional. Christ commands His followers to spread His redemption message throughout the world.

Christians often refer to this assignment as the Great Commission. It is a mammoth task. No one who takes Christ's last words seriously need ever feel bored or underchallenged. Unless we mothers relate our lives to God's Great Commission, no matter how noble our goals for ourselves and our children, we will miss the mark if we fail to experience this redemption personally and involve our lives in helping others experience it.

However, we sometimes view our children as a hindrance to our involvement in God's plan. Anyone who has tried to lead a Bible study while keeping a toddler entertained or to counsel a distraught friend while a baby cries in the background knows how difficult it can be. We need to remind ourselves and each other that our family *is* our primary ministry and not a frustrating obstacle to "real" ministry.

One night when Roger was away, sickness hit one child and pinworms another. Between the two maladies, I was up sixteen times that night. (Yes, I counted!) My fatigue the next day didn't alter the need to follow the doctor's orders for ridding our household of pinworms.

Besides giving medication, every day for a week I had to change all the beds, wash all the pajamas, and vacuum all the floors.

One evening that week I was to speak to a group of college and career women. I had planned to use that day to refine my notes and work on visual aids, but the day wasn't long enough to include washing clothes, changing beds, vacuuming floors, plus the everyday jobs (meals, caring for the children, telephone calls), and still have time left to work on my talk. I felt torn and divided. Before I came to the place where I could laugh, I cried.

Experiences like this are commonplace in the life of every mother. It is easy to feel frustrated by the seemingly conflicting demands of children and ministry to those outside the home. Reaching the world for Christ with a toddler hanging on your skirts isn't easy. Our children may seem to keep us from the spiritual outreach we feel God and others expect of us. This produces frustration and resentment. Our children may seem to be a roadblock, or at least a detour, keeping us back from real work for Christ.

Much of this frustration can be eased when we realize the family is an important part of God's strategy for propagating the faith and redeeming a people for Himself. In our zeal, perhaps we have overlooked the potential disciples in our midst. We may have also neglected the impact families can have through family-to-family evangelism and discipling.

TEACHING OUR CHILDREN

God commands us to minister to our children.

> "Do not forget the things your eyes have seen or let them slip from your heart as long as you live. Teach

31

them to your children and to their children after
them . . . so that you, your children and their children after them may fear the Lord your God as long
as you live by keeping all his decrees and commands
that I give you, and so that you may enjoy long life.
. . . These commandments that I give you today are
to be upon your hearts. Impress them on your children. Talk about them when you sit at home and
when you walk along the road, when you lie down
and when you get up." (Deuteronomy 4:9, 6:2,6-7)

God commands us to teach our children and even
our grandchildren about Him, so that they will teach
their children to also teach their children—establishing
a chain of truth from generation to generation. As the
psalmist writes,

He commanded our forefathers to teach their children, so the next generation would know . . . even
the children yet to be born, and they in turn would
tell their children. Then they would put their trust
in God and would not forget his deeds but would
keep his commands. They would not be like their
forefathers—a stubborn and rebellious generation,
whose hearts were not loyal to God, whose spirits
were not faithful to him. (Psalm 78:5-8)

God loves to see a family serving Him faithfully for
generations.

He used the Recabites as one example of generations
who obeyed their earthly father, and contrasted this with
Israel's disobedience to their heavenly Father. The Recabites' obedience for generations pleased God. He
blessed them because of their unswerving faithfulness
to the commands of their ancestor: "The descendants of

Jonadab son of Recab have carried out the command their forefather gave them" (Jeremiah 35:16). But He chided Israel, "Will you not learn a lesson and obey my words?" (Jeremiah 35:13). God still longs for generations to follow Him as zealously as the Recabites followed their forefather.

One important family chain of obedience to God that the New Testament mentions includes a grandmother, mother, and son. Paul wrote about this godly heritage to Timothy: "I have been reminded of your sincere faith, which first lived in your grandmother Lois and in your mother Eunice and, I am persuaded, now lives in you also" (2 Timothy 1:5). Timothy was blessed to have a grandmother and mother who were examples of faith in Christ and who taught him the Scriptures from infancy (2 Timothy 3:15).

Two New Testament letters were written to Timothy, but we know little about his grandmother Lois or his mother Eunice. All we know for sure is that God credited them for their part in transmitting a living faith to Timothy. Even if they had no public ministry of their own, they greatly contributed to the cause of Christ through Timothy.

YOUR FISHING NET

When I think of multiplying my life spiritually through my children, my mind races with the possibilities. I have asked God to make our family a chain of the faithful until Christ comes again. I pray that my children will all love God and walk faithfully with Him. Since they were babies I have prayed for God's choice of marriage partners for them. I pray for their children, and their children's children—that all would be ardent in their devotion to Christ and fruitful in touching lives for Him.

But as I visualize it, I've decided that a chain doesn't portray the idea well. A fishing net is much better! Chains bind people, but nets catch people, and Jesus said He would make us fishers of men (Matthew 4:19). Imagine your family's net starting with you and your husband—or with your parents or grandparents if they were followers of Christ—and enlarging as you add children and grandchildren. Picture countless people rescued by Christ through your family net.

Mothering can seem an isolated occupation unrelated to anything beyond the immediate needs of the family, but there is no more natural way for a mother to influence her world for Christ than through her own children. We will touch few lives with more intensity than the children God has placed in our homes. The implications of this are awesome.

Time devoted to our children should not be spent marking time, but as an investment in one of our greatest ministry opportunities. Although our children should not be the total focus of our lives, if we neglect them to pursue other opportunities we may one day find we lacked a biblical vision of mothering.

DEVELOPING OUR VISION

If commitment to our role as a mother languishes, this may be true not because the job is too small or unchallenging but because our vision is too small. Our dreams for our task may be thin and weak. We fail to hear God's call and miss the broad scope of the possibilities before us. We focus instead on the routine activities and demands—changing diapers, potty training, cleaning up messes, telling the kids for the fifth time not to slam the door—and miss any sense of a higher calling.

Mothers, look up and look ahead! Ask yourself: In five, ten, twenty, even forty years, what will I wish that I had done today? We want to avoid reaching the end of our lives with regret. Look ahead, decide what is really important, and plan to live accordingly.

Solomon wrote, "A prudent man sees danger and takes refuge, but the simple keep going and suffer for it" (Proverbs 22:3). He repeated this saying in Proverbs 27:12. Perhaps Solomon repeated this proverb because too few of us look ahead, assess our situation, and change direction when necessary.

Several years ago, I heard a dedicated missionary share what she would do differently if she could start raising her family again. This woman was committed to Christ and his cause, and she spent her life serving others—so the depth and quality of her life made me sit up and listen when she shared. She said she would stay home more, be kinder to her children, and feed them spiritually.

Stay Home More

Even knowing she would spend almost all of her married life as a missionary in Asia, this woman said she would have postponed full-time language study—which took her away from her children during their preschool years—until she could do it without being gone from her children.

I too am jealous for the influence I have at this crucial period in my child's life to teach him what is good, to enrich his life with beauty, to train him in obedience and respect, to stimulate his eager intellect, to encourage his attempts to try new things, and to play with him. I want to enjoy these years that happen only once and are soon gone forever.

BE KINDER

We can all identify with the missionary's desire to be kinder to her children—kinder in our speech, and more gentle in our touch.

Perhaps nothing stirs this desire more than observing an unkind mother. You know the supermarket scene: A mother battles with an impossible budget, a shopping cart with a bent wheel, and three young children. One is riding in the grocery cart pulling things off the shelves, one is trailing along by clinging to her skirt, and the third is eating from a box of Captain Crunch the mother had not planned to buy.

When the mother finally sees the third child elbow-deep in Captain Crunch and trailing sugary morsels in her wake, she lets out a scream. She shakes her daughter and berates her with a string of harsh and cruel words. The turbulent stream of unkind words echoes down the aisle.

I identify with her frustrations, but my heart is smitten. I long to become more kind in my reactions toward my own children.

FEED THEM SPIRITUALLY

Our days are full of opportunities to share spiritual truth with our children. We can use everyday incidents as a springboard for this. We can explain how Jesus washed away our sins as we give them a bath, or talk about the parable of the good soil as we work in the garden, or tell them Jesus knows the number of hairs on their head as we comb their hair. Making or slicing bread can be the setting for telling them that Jesus is the bread of life, or that man doesn't live by bread alone, or how Jesus fed five thousand people with two loaves of bread and five fishes. Seeds of truth are waiting everywhere to be planted in your child's mind. But you must be there to plant those seeds.

An Evaluation

Perhaps we should evaluate our mothering. Ask yourself these questions:

Do I have a constructive, long-range vision for my children? Am I exercising intelligent foresight? Or will I wake up one morning lamenting,

"I wish I had spent more time with my kids!"

"If only I had given more thought to their spiritual training."

"I wish I had listened to them more carefully."

"I'm sorry I didn't enjoy them more while they were home."

"I wish I'd been kinder."

"I'm sorry I was gone so much."

It is true that we cannot redo or undo what we've already done. Our past mistakes and neglects can't be eradicated, nor can all of the present consequences of our sins be erased. But we can ask God to forgive us and to raise something beautiful from the ashes of our mistakes. It may be too late for *us* to have an influence in our grown children's lives, but God can work quite apart from us. He may use others. He may allow us to have a part only through prayer, but it's never too late for God. Let these words from a sermon called "Needless Regrets" by John Henry Jowett encourage you:

And even supposing we have made mistakes, and we would dearly like to have the choice back again that we might take the other turning, what then?

37

Who is our God? And what are His name and character? Cannot He knit up the raveled bit of work, and in His own infinitely gracious way make it whole again? With all our mistakes we may throw ourselves upon His inexhaustible goodness, and say with Saint Teresa, "Undertake Thou for me, O Lord."

It is the very gospel of His grace that He can repair the things that are broken. He can reset the joints of the bruised reed. He can restore the broken heart. He can deal with the broken vow. And if He can do all this, can He not deal with our mistakes? If unknowingly we went astray and took the wrong turning, will not His infinite love correct our mistakes, and make the crooked straight?[2]

QUESTIONS FOR REFLECTION OR DISCUSSION

1. Look to the future. Twenty years from now what will you wish you had done today? What are you doing today that will give you peace twenty years from now?
2. If you made a list of three things you'd like to do differently, what would you include?
3. Reread Jowett's words on "Needless Regrets" and in prayer offer your regrets to God. Ask Him to set things straight, to bring healing, etc.
4. Of the following, choose one and write out a specific plan for application:
   a. Teach my children what is good
   b. Enrich their lives with beauty
   c. Train them in obedience and respect
   d. Stimulate their interests
   e. Encourage them to attempt new things
   f. Pray with them

NOTES
1. Arthur Porrit, *John Henry Jowett* (New York: Hodder & Stoughton, 1900), p. 4.
2. John Henry Jowett, *Things That Matter Most* (New York: Revell, 1913), p. 206.

Chapter Three

WHAT VALUES ARE
REALLY IMPORTANT?

"**M**y life is ruined," the man cried out in anguish to the counselor. "I've lost my wife and children! How can you say I'm successful?"

Raised by a widowed mother in extreme poverty, he had vowed as a young man that he would make something of himself. One day he would provide a nice home and financial security for his mother. His own family would live in a fine home, his children would attend the best schools, and his family would never know financial want of any kind.

But now he was desperately unhappy. His wife had filed for divorce, and the children sided with her. How could this counselor say he was successful?

"You are a successful man. You can be very proud of yourself. You have achieved your goals," the counselor replied. "Your goals were to provide financially for your mother, wife, and children. You achieved those goals. You are a success. But you are miserable too, because you chose the wrong goals."

This man's problem was his materialistic value

41

system. Eminently successful financially, he was a failure in the truly important areas of life. His wife was divorcing him because she had wanted him, not his money. He would never admit he rated financial security above his family in importance, but he was deceived. His actions spoke for themselves. He lived for the wrong goals and by the wrong values, and he had alienated his family without wanting to.

Mothers, we too may delude ourselves about our values. We may be just as much out of touch as this man was. We may achieve our goals and receive accolades, but live with regret later because we chose to be successful in the wrong areas.

Effective mothering is a matter of values. Our values tell us what is important, worthwhile, and desirable. Our values, like an ever-present pair of tinted eyeglasses, color life for us. Our values influence our decisions, our goals, our thoughts, and the way we spend our time and money.

Because our values so crucially influence the direction and quality of our lives, it is important for us to identify and change our values if necessary.

BEGIN WITH GOD

A proper value system must begin with God. Our Creator knows what has true value. He hasn't abandoned us. He hasn't left us without any help or direction. We do not need to live randomly or vaguely.

God provided the Bible to give us direction and wisdom in this. Just as an optician grinds the lenses of eyeglasses to correct and sharpen our vision, so the regular reading, personal study, and practical application of the Bible will shape our convictions about what has lasting value.

As you read the Bible, ask God,

"What do You value, Lord?"

"Do I value what You value?"

"What changes must I make to live more consistently with Your values, Lord?"

God Values Relationships

God values our relationship with Him and our relationships with others. The Ten Commandments present His value system. The first four commandments deal with our relationship to God, and the next six concern our relationships with other people.

In the New Testament, a law professor asked Jesus which commandment was the most important. Jesus replied that the most important was to love God, and the next most important was to love our neighbor (Mark 12:29-31).

Do you value relationships? Is your relationship with God supremely important? Do you spend daily time reading the Bible and praying—inviting God to speak to you, and talking to Him as well? Quality communication is essential to developing any effective relationship, especially our relationship with God. A daily devotional time is like having a date with God. It is a time to get to know Him and to enjoy His company.

Do you do what God tells you to do? Obedience is essential for a deepening relationship with God. God says, "If you love me, you will obey what I command" (John 14:15). God does not demand perfection, but He requires deliberate, step-by-step acts of obedience from us.

What occupies your thoughts? If we value a relationship with God, we should develop new thought patterns. "Since, then, you have been raised with Christ, set your hearts on things above, where Christ is seated at the right hand of God. Set your minds on things above, not on earthly things" (Colossians 3:1-2). Center your thoughts on God by interacting with Him throughout the day.

God also places high value on our relationships with other people. He says we are to love others as we love ourselves (Matthew 22:39). Careful study of the New Testament gives insight into how to develop better relationships.

A visitor scolded a missionary in Korea who grew lovely roses because he let his sons play in his rose garden. "I'm raising boys, not roses," the missionary observed. He understood God's values. People—and our relationships with them—are more important than things.

My husband's Aunt Barbara lives in a home for mentally retarded women. Roger was concerned because it was difficult to monitor her situation, so we planned a trip to familiarize ourselves with the home. We were totally unprepared for what we found.

In a large white house in a tiny Florida town, twenty-two women live with A.W. and Bertha Gaskins, a middle-aged Christian couple. We hoped to find a clean home run by kind, caring people. What we found far exceeded our expectations. Mr. and Mrs. Gaskins, who had prayed for five years to be able to operate a home for women from state mental institutions, now give these women a level of loving care that few parents provide for their own children.

After breakfast on Sunday mornings the women line up eagerly outside the dining room. Bertha fixes each woman's hair and applies powder and lipstick. Although the women wait their turn, this is no assembly-line operation. Each woman receives Bertha's full attention. The shade of lipstick chosen flatters each woman's complexion and outfit. Bertha talks kindly and upliftingly to each one: "Darling, you look beautiful. Mama loves you. Run upstairs and get the necklace Mama bought for you. Your dress needs something at the neck." Then each woman leaves for church looking attractive and feeling loved.

A. W. and Bertha Gaskins believe these women are important and maintain a loving relationship with each of them. Their lives demonstrate that they believe people are important.

Do you value relationships with people? What are you doing to develop your relationship with your husband and children? Are they more important than things? Do you value your children more than your living room furniture, more than your career, and more than your rose garden?

God Values Character

Especially in the way He values godly character, God's value system is radically different from our own. We value power and position. God says, "Whoever wants to become great among you must be your servant, and whoever wants to be first must be your slave" (Matthew 20:26-27).

We value physical beauty. God says, "Do not consider his appearance or his height, for I have rejected him. The Lord does not look at the things man looks at. Man looks at the outward appearance, but the Lord looks at the heart" (1 Samuel 16:7).

God turns man's value system upside down. "What is highly valued among men is detestable in God's sight" (Luke 16:15).

Man cares about externals, but God cares about inner qualities. Man values beauty, brains, wealth, and power; God values a pure heart.

Integrity and faithfulness have greater value to God than success. He says, "The unfading beauty of a gentle and quiet spirit" is of greater worth than a pretty face and nice clothes (1 Peter 3:4). It is more important to be beautiful inside than outside.

What are your goals for yourself and your children? Are they outstanding beauty, intellectual accomplishments, athletic ability, social status, or power goals? Or are they inner character goals?

TIME WITH OUR CHILDREN

One gauge of our values is the amount of time we spend with our children. Dr. Howard Hendricks, former professor of Christian education at Dallas Theological Seminary and a counselor of many parents, says he has never heard parents say they regretted spending too much time with their children.

Few parents would disagree that spending time with our children is important. But recent findings reveal how very important time with our children is, and how early it should begin. Richard M. Restak, author of *The Brain: The Last Frontier,* reveals that in one section of the brain, cell growth in infants is stimulated by snuggling, rocking, and cuddling. Restak observes:

> With few exceptions, societies which provide infants with a great deal of physical affection and bodily contact produce relatively nonviolent adults. Physical holding and carrying of the infant turns out to be the most important factor responsible for the infant's normal mental and social development.[1]

Selma Fraiberg in *Every Child's Birthright: In Defense of Mothering* discusses these concerns:

> I worry about babies and small children who are delivered like packages to neighbors, to strangers, to storage houses like Merry Mites. In the years when a baby and his parents make their first enduring human partnerships, when love, trust, joy, and self-evaluation emerge through the nurturing love of human partners, millions of small children in our land may be learning values for survival in our baby banks. They may learn the rude justice of the communal playpen. They may learn that the world outside the home is an indifferent world, or even a hostile world. Or they may learn that all adults are interchangeable, that love is capricious, that human attachment is a perilous investment, and that love should be hoarded for the self in the service of survival.[2]

Fraiberg contends that children reared without an enduring relationship with a mother figure seem incapable of sustaining lasting relationships later in life. Will our society's disenchantment with the full-time mother worsen our soaring divorce rates?

I can't help wondering if the absent, preoccupied, or apathetic mother hasn't left a greater void than we recognize.

QUALITY VERSUS QUANTITY

I cringe when I hear, "It isn't how much time you spend with your children that matters, but whether the time you do spend is of high quality." High quality for whom?

47

If we define quality time as that which meets a need, we must ask, "Meets a need for whom?" Quality time for a four-year-old may be having Mommie there to kiss a scrape and apply a bandage. A nine-year-old may consider it quality time if Mom is available to talk as soon as he bursts through the front door after school.

One morning our five-year-old Matthew ran into the house calling, "Mommie, Mommie, come quick!"

Visions of an accident or catastrophe raced through my mind. I wondered what I would find as he hurriedly led me out the back door.

Then he put his finger to his mouth and pointed to the most wildly beautiful butterfly I've ever seen. Together we shared a magical moment. That was quality time.

Quality time for our children often defies advance scheduling. We may fool ourselves to think that quality time is time scheduled for our convenience. But we won't fool our children. We cannot afford to neglect the everyday "being-there" experiences and hope to make up the difference with occasional times conveniently scheduled in the future.

One evening last summer I sat on our deck with the manuscript of this book spread out, struggling to find ideas and words to adequately communicate my concerns. Finally, after some frustration, a breakthrough came. My thoughts crystallized and I began writing feverishly.

In the midst of my writing, my daughter, Beth, came out to talk. She had just watched an episode of "Little House on the Prairie" and wanted to talk about how the parents in the show handled an incident. The story was ripe in her mind. She had to ask her questions and share her observations right away. So I set aside my writing and gave her my full attention. As we talked I sensed the richness of this time for Beth. After ten or fifteen minutes, I returned to my pen and paper wondering if our talk would have had the same quality if I had asked her to save it until bedtime. Would we have captured the same intensity?

Are you there to hold your child close when someone hurts his feelings, or to listen to something funny that happened in class, or to carry on a spontaneous conversation in the kitchen after school?

While we lived in Arizona, Roger planned a one-hour date with each child every week. The children could decide how to spend their times with Dad. Finances were tight, so we hoped they wouldn't all want to go out for sundaes or pancakes.

But they rarely asked for anything that cost money. Matt and Roger went to the library to draw sailing ships. Beth asked Roger to pull her up and down the sidewalk on her roller skates. Graham and Roger played with toy trucks in the sand dunes at the end of our street. These dates were not exotic, expensive, or too time-consuming, but the children deemed them quality times. Sometimes quality time is the memory of many brief but enjoyable occasions like those simple dates with Dad.

When was the last time you read a story to your child, or picked up your baby to snuggle and play when it wasn't time to feed or diaper him? How long has it been since you sat on the floor and played dolls or pushed little trucks around? Or spent an extra long time sitting on your child's bed and talking?

Resist the temptation to make the television or the baby swing your baby-sitter. Do not anesthetize your child for your temporary convenience instead of personally meeting his needs. We have many mechanisms for entertaining our children, but sitting them on our laps and reading them a story is infinitely better than having them sit beside a tape player to hear that same story. Mechanical substitutes may supplement our personal involvement, but they should never replace us.

"Desire accomplished is sweet to the soul" (Proverbs 13:19, KJV). But unless our desires come from sound values, we may experience bitterness rather than sweetness. I began to realize this when God made me aware of three spoilers in my life.

INSTANT SATISFACTION

The spoiler called "instant satisfaction" surfaced clearly one day when I stopped to evaluate why some days ended in satisfaction while others ended with a vague sense of dissipation and discouragement.

Finally, it dawned on me that "good" days were those days when I scratched lots off my "do list." "Bad" days were those days when I could show few tangible results for my day's efforts.

Frustration peaked on bad days just before dinner—when Roger, and the young men living with us for training in Christian discipleship, came home. If the house was a mess, my pride shook her finger and scolded: "They'll think you didn't do a thing all day. What do you have to show for your day? Nothing!"

True, I had nothing visible to show for my day. But I had spent time with God; I had focused attention on my children; I had made people more important than accomplishing tasks. I had attempted to live by God's values. As I reflected on my "good-days, bad-days syndrome" a startling revelation surfaced: *I realized that if I lived my life for what made me feel good at the end of each day I would give my life to things of secondary importance.*

I must constantly remind myself that though the visible, tangible world is so insistent and clamorous in its demands, I must not let it badger me into spending my life unwisely. The results of living by God's value system aren't immediately apparent like clean windows or a newly papered wall. But years from now, by God's grace, my time with God and my children will produce results brighter than sparkling windows. I must take the long view. I must choose to do those things that will give satisfaction as I view my life as a whole, rather than measure satisfaction at the end of each day.

Housework is only one area where instant satisfaction robs us of what has lasting value. Our activities may be excellent in themselves. Christian activities, careers, hobbies, and crafts may furnish recognition, esteem, and fulfillment—but will the sweetness of instant satisfaction turn to bitterness in the years ahead?

Satisfaction seldom comes instantly in mothering. Children rarely pat you on the back and say, "Mom, I really appreciate your wisdom and your daily sacrifices. You have truly enriched my life and helped me grow. I'm sure grateful for all you do." If we are to keep going as mothers we need to be motivated by an inner conviction of what is truly important.

Now is the time to get things done . . .
    wade in the water,
    sit in the sun,
    squish my toes
    in the mud by the door,
explore the world in a boy just four.

Now is the time to study books,
    flowers,
    snails,
    how a cloud looks;

to ponder "up,"
where God sleeps nights,
why mosquitoes take such big bites.

Later there'll be time
to sew and clean,
paint the hall
that soft new green,
to make new drapes,
refinish the floor—
Later on . . . when he's not just four.
Irene Foster, "Time Is of the Essence"

THE GOOD LIFE

The "good life" is my second spoiler.

Four hundred years before the birth of Christ, Socrates voiced this concern about values in his day:

Could I climb the highest place in Athens, I would lift up my voice and proclaim, "Fellow citizens, why do you turn and scrape every stone to gather wealth, and take so little care of your children to whom you must one day relinquish all?"

Recently I heard a lovely, sad-eyed teenager express her frustration: "Why does my mother want to take me shopping to buy something when I'm depressed? What I want is for her to hug me." And during a parenting seminar, another teen exclaimed, "Why do parents stop kissing us when we become teenagers?"

Are we guilty of giving our children everything but ourselves? What values are we communicating?

Audrey, Joan, and Marta have each decided to work outside their homes. Each bases her decision to work on what she feels will benefit her children. Audrey says she must work to make it financially.

Her children, ages nine and eleven, are bright. But a college education seems an impossibility on her husband's salary alone. So Audrey works for their good—their future.

Joan grew up in a poor family. All her clothes were hand-me-downs. She vowed her children would never wear seconds, so she works to give her children what she missed as a child. Her children are five, six, and twelve.

Marta works to have enough tuition money to send her school-age children to a Christian school. She regrets having the neighbors care for her eleven-month-old daughter, but feels the sacrifice is worth it.

The decisions these mothers made are based on their values. By working, each feels she will benefit her children. Each of these women must judge whether her absence really benefits her family. Audrey, Joan, and Marta must confront the question, *Is money for college, nice things, or a Christian education more valuable than my being there?* Each family must come to grips with the issues and the alternatives. They should weigh the pros and cons, and make their decision in light of biblical values.

In this process, these questions might help:

Does my absence mean someone else will care for my children? How long will they be under another's care each day? Is this the person I want to raise and influence my child in my place? How many surrogate mothers will be involved over the years? What impact will that have?

Does my job sap my energies so that I am tired and pressured and unable to give them quality time? Are my creativity, my wit, and my best efforts spent outside my family? Do they get only the leftovers?

A sentence from Psalm 101 has been both

challenging and convicting for me: "I will walk in my house with blameless heart" (Psalm 101:2). When God speaks to me about being more loving, this verse reminds me to make application in my family first—and then to others. It forces me to ask, "Am I more spiritual, more loving, or more fun somewhere else? Who gets my best—my family or others?"

> We give of ourselves when we give gifts of the heart—love, kindness, joy, understanding, sympathy, tolerance, forgiveness.
>
> We give of ourselves when we give gifts of the mind—ideas, dreams, purposes, ideals, principles, plans, inventions, projects, poetry.
>
> We give of ourselves when we give gifts of words—encouragement, inspiration, guidance.
>
> Emerson said it well—"Rings and jewels are not gifts, but apologies for gifts. The only true gift is a portion of thyself."
>
> Wilfred A. Peterson, "The Art of Giving"

PRESSURES

I began waking at 3:30, unable to sleep, my mind whirling with to do lists, current attractions, coming events, and deadlines. Sometimes I lay in bed praying, committing these details to God. At other times I got up, made lists, and did a few things before returning to bed. While the children were at school, I zipped around trying to keep ahead of the rapidly accumulating work.

During this time I became painfully aware of the harsh tone of my voice in my dealings with the children. I felt a stab of anguish each time I answered sharply.

I talked about this with a friend. "Wouldn't it be ironic," she said, "to write a book about mothering while being cross with your kids?" Her pithy reply served as a pointed reminder again and again.

Writing was only part of the pressure I felt, but it was a part. So I decided to put it aside until the other pressures subsided. Pressures are my third spoiler.

My friend's comment has a core of truth applicable to many situations. For example, have you ever been trying to get the house pulled together because company was coming—and the children seemed bent on nullifying your efforts? I think you know what I mean. You've just mopped the floor and someone tracks through leaving grass clippings and leaves everywhere. Or you step into the bathroom to light a candle, and discover the children giving the dog his annual bath.

How easy to allow the pressure of company to determine my values. My guests will be here only for a few hours, but I will live with my children many years. So I've decided not to let what company thinks of my housekeeping or hostessing become more important than "walking blamelessly in my own house."

Finding the Balance

I've strongly stated the case for spending time with our children because this emphasis is needed today. However, certain balancing statements must also be made.

1. *A mother's world must not revolve only around her children.* Children are not more important than God—or our husbands.

For their own well-being and the well-being of your marriage, children must understand that they come after your spouse. They need to know they fit into a secure place within an established set of relationships. This will help them develop a Christian concept of marriage.

The rash of divorces now occurring after children leave the nest accentuates the need for continuing to build the marriage relationship above all other human relationships.

2. *Children are more important than housework, but parents must still do their work.* While we want our children to know that they are more important than the house, we also want them to learn that everyone has work to do. We want them to remember a diligent, hard-working mother who enjoyed her responsibilities. She didn't always drop what she was doing to play. Children must also learn how to wait patiently.

3. *Mother is a person too.* Children need to know that our strength and endurance are not limitless. Mothers do not exist solely for their children's benefit. They need and deserve time for themselves.

PAYING THE PRICE

It is not enough to simply discern what has value. We must pay a price to make those values ours. Everything has a price. Nothing is free.

"But salvation is a free gift," you may say. True, but Jesus paid the price.

Somebody always pays a price. Every victory and every success comes at the expense of something or someone. Roger Hull observes, "Some people treat life like a slot machine, trying to put in as little as possible and hoping to hit a jackpot. Wiser people think of life as a solid investment from which they receive in terms of what they put in."[3]

Almost every Christian parent wants to have their children honor God as they mature. But we may expect the product without being willing to involve ourselves in the process. Do we value our children enough to pay the price?

Roger's dates with our children rarely cost any money. But they cost some time. Roger is a busy man and opportunities always exceed the time available. Like all of us, he must decide what to give his time to and what to leave undone.

When I laid aside my writing to talk with my daughter, I paid a price. I lost momentum in my writing, but it was worth the cost. I value my time with my children above my writing.

One spring, as the end of the school year approached, my concern deepened. I felt disturbed about the signs of negative peer influence in my children's lives. I observed attitudes and actions that troubled me.

Peer influence is a natural part of growing up. Shielding our children from every unfavorable influence is not only impossible, but also undesirable. But, as summer approached, I wondered how I could use the vacation to draw them closer under my influence again.

I knew it wouldn't be easy. In the summer our doorbell rang all day long. Our home was the hub of the neighborhood. I knew I must plan an interesting and active summer so my children wouldn't miss playing with their friends so much. Could I control the amount of time spent with friends and ensure that ours was the place of primary influence? I knew I would have to plan a tight schedule to make it work.

I shared my concerns with Georgia, a mother I deeply respect. "I've thought of taking them swimming after they get their chores done and planning crafts for the afternoons," I told her. "I figure if I plan a full schedule it will be easier to control the amount of time they play with others. Then when neighbor kids come to the door, I'll invite them to come back at 3:30."

Georgia challenged me with one short sentence: "Jeanie, you have to *make* it happen."

Her words often remind me that it isn't the creative ideas or the great insights that lie at the heart of mothering, but the mother's commitment and willingness to pay the price. She must be willing to invest time in cultivating a heart and lifestyle that will make her values a reality in the lives of her children.

Life is so short. What will you value?

Time is so limited. What will you value?

We mothers can accomplish only so much. What will we value?

QUESTIONS FOR REFLECTION OR DISCUSSION

1. The Bible gives us a knowledge of what God values. What creative ideas do you have to make Bible reading a part of your busy life so that you can learn to value what God values?
2. What five areas in your life do you want to succeed in?
3. What times this past week do you think your child would consider quality time with you?
4. What areas of instant satisfaction threaten to keep you from living by what God says is important?

NOTES

1. Richard M. Restak, *The Brain: The Last Frontier,* as quoted in *The Evangelical Newsletter.*
2. Selma Fraiberg, *Every Child's Birthright: In Defense of Mothering* (New York: Bantam Books, 1978), pp. 129-130.
3. Roger Hull, as quoted in "Points To Ponder," *Reader's Digest,* August, 1979, p. 20.

Chapter Four

START WITH YOURSELF

The single most important decision a mother can make is to develop her own life with God. Unless she nurtures herself spiritually first, she will have no base from which to have a positive spiritual influence on her children.

As Billy Graham wrote, women should first "cultivate their souls that in turn they may cultivate the souls of their children."

Scripture reveals God's agenda for making a spiritual impact on our children: We must begin with ourselves; then we must teach our children. We will better understand our responsibility as mothers if we follow this order.

In Deuteronomy 6:6-7, God first tells parents, "These commandments that I give you today are to be upon your hearts." Then he says, "Impress them on your children." Before He tells us to teach, God tells us to grow.

God wants us to start with ourselves.

BE A DOER AND A TEACHER

Ezra illustrates the approach of being a doer first and then a teacher: "For Ezra had devoted himself to the

59

study and observance of the Law of the Lord, and to teaching its decrees and laws in Israel" (Ezra 7:10). He studied God's Word, applied it to his own life, then taught others. The suggested order is: Study, Do, Teach.

Our Lord Jesus Christ exemplified this order in His own life and ministry. Luke said he wrote in his gospel "about all that Jesus began *to do* and *to teach*" (Acts 1:1).

Jesus lived what He taught, and taught what He lived. His life perfectly mirrored all that He spoke. His teachings amaze us, but His life brings us to our knees.

Jesus Himself confirmed the importance of doing and teaching when He said,

> "Anyone who breaks one of the least of these commandments and teaches others to do the same will be called least in the kingdom of heaven, but whoever practices and teaches these commands will be called great in the kingdom of heaven."
>
> (Matthew 5:19)

Notice the key words *practices* and *teaches*. God expects us to first put ourselves under the authority of His Word *before* we teach it to others. God's Word must have an impact in our lives first, and then we may minister it to our children. The Holy Scriptures were given as words to be obeyed by all.

A young man named Jerry applied to a Christian college but was not accepted. Confused, he asked my husband for counsel. Jerry found it difficult to explain his situation because his parents told him not to tell anyone that he hadn't been accepted—but to say instead that he decided to join the Air Force. Jerry's parents had taught him the importance of honesty. His father was a pastor. But now Jerry struggled with the inconsistency between how his parents lived and what they taught.

As parents, what we *are* makes a greater impact on our children than what we *teach*.

Think for a moment: Why does God insist on the order of doing first, then teaching?

GOD CARES FOR INDIVIDUALS

First, God is concerned about *me*. He is the God of the individual. The Christian life must be entered into and developed at the *personal* level. One does not become a Christian by being born of Christian parents, regularly attending church, or by hanging around "spiritual" believers. New birth comes to people one by one, and so does the development of this new life. It comes by decisions and commitments made one at a time on a personal level.

God cares about me as an individual and will one day judge me as an individual. "For we must all appear before the judgment seat of Christ" (2 Corinthians 5:10). On that day we will be stripped of our roles and labels. "Each of us will give an account of himself to God" (Romans 14:12).

We will stand before God—not as "Molly the wife," or "Molly the mother," or "Molly the bank teller," but just "Molly." God will look at our relationship with Him before examining our service for Him. His order is to do first, and then to teach.

Knowing we will stand before God demands personal reflection and evaluation. When I stand before Him, what measure will He use to judge me? What is His standard? What is His goal?

GOD'S GOAL: CHRISTLIKENESS

Another reason we should start with ourselves is that God's plan has always been for people to become like Him. Christlikeness is His goal for us. We will be "measured by nothing less than the full stature of Christ" (Ephesians 4:13, *New English Bible*).

Adam and Eve were created in God's image, but they disobeyed God and marred that likeness. Ever since then we have all sinned, and we are but warped representations of what God originally created.

Our heartiest efforts will never recover that prized condition—Godlikeness. But Christ left the glory of heaven, became a man, and died on the cross for us. Christ's death was an exchange and a substitution: His life for mine. And now He is alive, and lives inside us through his Spirit. All this is because God still wants us to be like Him. He wants us to demonstrate His values in both our doing and our teaching.

We are to gradually become more and more like Christ in our inner life and character and in the values we express—in thought, word, and deed.

When my children were younger they liked to pretend they were animals—especially dogs. They crawled around barking, wagging their tails, and lapping water from a bowl. But despite their attention to details like scratching imaginary fleas, they were not dogs.

Likewise, no one becomes a child of God by merely acting like one outwardly. He must be reborn spiritually into God's family. "Flesh gives birth to flesh, but the Spirit gives birth to spirit. You should not be surprised at my saying, 'You must be born again'" (John 3:6-7).

We must have Christ's life in us. The Holy Spirit can then renew us within, and help us discern God's value system. We begin inside ourselves.

Our Lives Influence Others

A third reason to follow God's order—practice before we teach—is that the way we live influences others. You *are* an influence, and so am I, whether we consciously accept this responsibility or not. This is part of God's plan. People learn by observation and imitation.

I'm watching some children—who are dressed in their parents' clothes—pushing a baby carriage and shuffling along in shoes too big, with adult-size hats bobbing over their eyes. Now, to sound grown-up, one speaks harshly to the doll in the baby carriage.

My heart sinks. Where in the world did they get the idea that parents talk like that? I wonder!

This could be overwhelmingly discouraging if negative characteristics were destined to go on endlessly. But God is in the business of breaking the chains of such destructive habits.

Breaking Chains

God delights in turning families in new directions by changing individuals. If you are already a Christian, you have been redeemed from the "empty way of life handed down to you from your forefathers" (1 Peter 1:18). He has already broken the destructive chain. The precious blood of Christ was the price God paid to break the chain and give you a new beginning. You can have a fresh start and a new life.

If you are not yet a Christian, then you can pray and personally invite Christ into your heart now. Listen to His gracious request: "Here I am! I stand at the door and knock. If anyone hears my voice and opens the door, I will go in and eat with him, and he with me" (Revelation 3:20). Once you have personally received Christ, you have begun life as a new person: "If anyone is in Christ, he is a new creation; the old has gone, the new has come!" (2 Corinthians 5:17).

A new chain can begin with you, with your children, and with your grandchildren. The Christlikeness of your chain will depend, in part, on the models you imitate and the model you become. Perhaps you are saying, "I want to change! But where do I start?"

START WITH YOURSELF

Every wise woman starts with herself. First, spend time every day reading the Bible and praying. This is essential to the cultivation of the Christ-life in you.

Second, be willing to respond to God when He makes you aware of areas in which you need to change.

When God points out sin in my life, my first reaction may be to argue defensively. One morning in my time with God, I sensed the Lord's rebuke as I read, "Reckless words pierce like a sword, but the tongue of the wise brings healing" (Proverbs 12:18).

"Me, Lord?" my disbelieving heart countered.

"Yes, Jean, you!"

Then God faithfully brought to mind recent examples from my life that illustrated my guilt: a disgusted tone of voice when one of the children didn't follow instructions, a sharp outburst when my patience had worn thin, a quick comment I wish I could have retracted. I needed to change.

I was jolted by seeing my own sinfulness. I was heartsick, but heartsickness can be constructive if it produces responsiveness to God. For "the Lord is close to the brokenhearted and saves those who are crushed in spirit" (Psalm 34:18).

God makes rich promises to those who are deeply sorry for their sin. "I live in a high and holy place, but also with him who is contrite and lowly in spirit, to revive the spirit of the lowly and to revive the heart of the contrite" (Isaiah 57:15). Jesus said, "Blessed are the poor in spirit, for theirs is the kingdom of heaven. Blessed are those who mourn, for they will be comforted" (Matthew 5:3-4). For those who are heartsick, God offers both hope and help. The hope God gives motivates us to change now.

> Now we are children of God, and what we will be has not yet been made known. But we know that when he appears, we shall be like him, for we shall see him as he is. Everyone who has this hope in him purifies himself, just as he is pure. (1 John 3:2-3)

And God's promise of help is something we can count on. "So do not fear, for I am with you; do not be dismayed, for I am your God. I will strengthen you and help you; I will uphold you with my righteous right hand" (Isaiah 41:10).

CHANGE IS A PROCESS

Although God is able to make dramatic changes in the lives of His children by performing immediate transformations, this is not His primary method of producing change in us. "Why not?" you ask. "Surely instantaneous change would be less painful for us, and more honoring to Him."

But God is our Father. Does an earthly father want his child to be born mature? What loving parent would want his children born as adults simply because it would spare them much time and trouble? After all, it would eliminate feedings at two A.M., dirty diapers, and windows broken by poorly aimed baseballs. You also wouldn't have to hold them on your lap, or tuck them in at night—but who would want to miss those experiences?

Our son Matt was once crawling toward a "no-no." Roger said, "Matt, no!" Then he watched as Matt stopped in his tracks. Roger could imagine the gears going around in Matt's mind, weighing the "I can do it," against his father's request for obedience. After a brief pause, Matt wheeled around and crawled to Roger and hugged him. His obedience brought tears to my husband's eyes.

In the same way, God enjoys observing our obedience and growth. He delights in experiencing the warmth of His Father-daughter relationship with us.

But we must not confuse being aware of God's will for us with *doing* His will. It is not enough to know what God wants of us as mothers. We must consciously enter into the process of being changed. Our part is to obey what He shows us to do.

My friend Karla is changing. She was distressed that her eight-year-old, Allan, was so bossy. She heard him ordering other children around whenever they came to play. He expected everyone to fall in line with his wishes. The other kids would endure only so much before they left in frustration. Karla recognized that unless Allan overcame his demanding behavior, he would be left virtually friendless.

Karla wondered how she could help Allan. She wondered, *Did Allan learn this attitude from me?* Did she sometimes sound like a drill sergeant? Were barking commands and expecting instant results her usual style?

In this way Karla began considering the relationship from her son's point of view. She was a no-nonsense person, and she did expect immediate obedience when she told Allan something. But she loved him and wanted to communicate a genuine concern for his best interest as well.

So she decided to start with herself and change her pattern of communication. But despite her genuine desire to change, she failed again and again. She prayed. She memorized appropriate verses of Scripture. Although she slowly saw some changes, it was a struggle to break established patterns. Often Karla called Allan over and apologized. "Allan, I'm sorry I spoke so sharply. Please keep praying with me that I will learn to speak more kindly."

Although Karla wanted to change and worked at it, she experienced only partial success—because change is usually a process that takes time as well as effort.

Then Karla made a wonderful discovery—change is a process in Allan's life too. She began wondering if she had sometimes been unreasonable in her expectations. Had she expected of him, a child, what even she could not do as a mature woman? Thinking like this helped Karla become more patient with Allan.

Karla still hasn't "arrived." Like all of us, she is still struggling, still learning how to obey God and let Him change her. But Karla started in the right place—with herself—and she has grown into a more understanding and more tolerant person. Her strenuous efforts are being rewarded.

God wants mothers to influence the children in our homes by our example as well as by our words. In our desire to have a positive impact on our children, we must remember the essential order—first do and then teach. We must always start with ourselves.

Drying the dishes one afternoon, I felt trapped. The children were being especially raucous, and I felt irritated. They seemed to rub against each other like sandpaper, and a tone of disharmony prevailed. "What's wrong with them?" I asked as I became more annoyed.

Then I paused and considered myself. Had I set the unpleasant tone? Had I been impatient and unkind in my dealings with them? Had I given them any undivided attention that day?

Gradually, I saw that I was not an innocent victim held captive by a bunch of hooligans. I was part of the problem, perhaps even the originator of the problem. How could I turn things around? I hung up my dish towel and focused my attention on them.

I gathered up several library books and a blanket, and we all climbed onto the couch and covered our legs with the blanket. I read to them for only half an hour, but the closeness and warmth changed the tone. No further action was necessary. I didn't have to correct or lecture them. It was enough to change my attitude.

To be wise, every woman must start with herself.

QUESTIONS FOR REFLECTION OR DISCUSSION

1. Why do you think God wants mothers to "start with themselves"?
2. What do you see in yourself that you don't want to pass on to your children and grandchildren?
3. In what ways does God help us become more like Jesus Christ?
4. What is one thing you might do this week to become more the woman God wants you to become and more the mother you want to become?

Chapter Five

GOD'S PART, MY PART

Six-and-a-half months into my first pregnancy, we moved to Seoul, South Korea. New sights, sounds, and smells alternately stimulated and numbed me: lovely Korean women sweeping by in long, brightly colored dresses; confusing and noisy traffic jams; taxi rides as breathtaking as any amusement park ride; and, saturating the air, the heavy, garlicky aroma of kimchi, a mainstay in the Korean diet—a fermented, spicy, pickled cabbage dish.

Culture shock! I had heard the term many times, and now I experienced it. After hours of shopping and sometimes bartering with the butcher, baker, and produce vendors, I returned home exhausted, put up my feet to relax, and stared at my very pregnant condition.

A couple of months later, after the Caesarean delivery of our son Matthew, I faced another adjustment—motherhood. As a first-time mother in a new country I observed many cultural differences in child care. Infants peeped out from beneath layers of quilts because the Koreans believed babies must be kept very warm. As soon as babies could hold their heads erect, they rode against their mother's back wrapped inside a blanket that encircled mother and baby, and was tied in place.

Initially some of the differences in child care were disconcerting, but then reassuring. It was encouraging to realize how sturdy babies must be since they survive various philosophies of child care throughout the world. I relaxed with the thought, *Our baby probably will make it, no matter whose philosophy I follow.*

But when it came to the spiritual and emotional aspects of mothering, that was a different matter. It would be foolish to view these areas as arbitrary. I had to know God's plan. I wanted to do what God wanted me to with this young life.

WAITING ON GOD—FOR CHILDREN

Before I was pregnant with Matthew, I studied the lives of biblical women who had waited for a child. These women were Sarah, the mother of Isaac; Hannah, the mother of Samuel; Rebekah, the mother of Jacob; Elizabeth, the mother of John the Baptist; and Samson's mother. From my study I gained a conviction that every child comes from God and ought to live for God's purposes.

Each of these women was initially barren. They waited and waited to conceive a child. Since failure to bear a child in their culture was often considered a curse, they experienced torment and ridicule. All of them endured a painful wait. Two of them—Sarah and Elizabeth—reached old age before conceiving.

Was it really necessary for these women to experience the agony of a long wait? Yes, there was a purpose.

God had something special in mind. He wanted to

give each of these mothers a special child—a child with a specific purpose—and He wanted to receive the glory. Everyone must know that God did it. The awe and wonder of conception is often lost on us, since almost anyone can conceive—rich or poor, educated or uneducated, godly or ungodly. We can easily forget the part God plays in every birth.

Unless a sense of wonder accompanies parenthood, we may either take our responsibility too lightly or else cling too tightly to our children. God knows that withholding children often produces a different mentality in a waiting mother- or father-to-be.

I wonder if Abraham could have laid his son Isaac on the altar if the long wait had not prepared his heart (see Genesis 22). Would Hannah have given her beloved young Samuel to God's service if he had come much earlier? Did the wait produce a conviction that Samuel came from God and should live for God's purposes, a conviction she otherwise might not have experienced?

Perhaps another reason God allowed these mothers to endure a long wait was to lay a groundwork of prayer. They knew that these children were children of purpose and promise, and undoubtedly each of them was much prayed for.

I too wanted the convictions of a mother who had waited on God, even though my wait was comparatively short. I prayed, "God, please give me the sense that these women had that this child will be from You and for You."

WHAT DOES GOD EXPECT OF MOTHERS?

After Matthew's birth, I realized that the child I held in my arms was not mine, not ours, but God's. He was a sacred charge—an assignment and heritage from God.

71

As I looked at him I asked, "What does God expect from me as a mother? What is my part and what is God's part in raising this child?"

Two verses helped me: "Unless the Lord builds the house, its builders labor in vain. Unless the Lord watches over the city, the watchmen stand guard in vain" (Psalm 127:1); and "The wise woman builds her house, but with her own hands the foolish one tears hers down" (Proverbs 14:1). Let's examine these verses more closely. What do they teach?

GOD'S PART

Unless God works, my best efforts are in vain. God must do the real work in my home. I cannot accomplish anything of spiritual and eternal value in the lives of my children. I can read everything written on child raising, closely supervise their activities, develop meaningful dialogue, and stay up late worrying—and still miss the target. I can toil and strive to the point of exhaustion, but unless God works, my efforts will be worthless. We can take them to church, but we can't make them worship. We can require Bible reading, but we can't make them enjoy doing it. We can provide an example, but we can't guarantee they will follow in our steps.

Henry Venn, an eighteenth century pastor, once wrote to a concerned widow about her son who had a greater appetite for pleasure than for God. Venn said that this painful experience should teach the mother about

> . . . your own weakness and inability to give a single ray of light, or to excite the faintest conviction of sin, or to communicate the least particle of spiritual good, to one who is dearer to you than life.

How ought this to take away every proud thought
of our own sufficiency, and to keep us earnest,
importunate suppliants at the door of the
Almighty's mercy and free grace.[1]

The best possible parenting cannot produce children who are spiritually responsive to God any more
than our witnessing can make people Christians. Something spiritual happens in a child's life because God has
done something. "Flesh gives birth to flesh, but the Spirit
gives birth to spirit" (John 3:6).

OUR PART

Knowing that God must work does not minimize our
responsibilities. In Psalm 127:1, Solomon doesn't suggest
that the builder neglect the building process, or that the
watchman desert his post—but only that their efforts
alone are not enough. The issue is faith, not desertion or
neglect. The watchman acknowledges that in the final
analysis God guards the city. The builder affirms that God
does the real building. The mother recognizes that only
God can make anything truly significant happen in her
child's life. The watchman must watch in faith, the
builder must build in faith, and the mother must mother
in faith. Our very best mothering—done in faith—is our
part.

Everywhere in Scripture we see that God invites
women and men to participate in His plans. He didn't
need Noah's skills, but He let him contribute a century of
ark-building labor. God commanded Moses to strike the
rock to provide a gushing flow of water for the people of
Israel. Certainly He didn't need Moses' assistance, but
God let him be involved.

MOTHERING AND DITCH-DIGGING

When Joram became king of Israel after the wicked reign of King Ahab, he faced a problem. King Mesha of Moab had paid tribute to Ahab, but he refused to recognize Joram. So Joram and his allies decided to cross the desert and surprise Mesha. But after a week's travel, they found themselves in deep trouble: no water. In desperation, they sought God's help.

"Is there a man of God around here?" they asked.

Elisha, God's prophet, gave them a word from the Lord to meet their need.

> Make this valley full of ditches. For this is what the Lord says: You will see neither wind nor rain, yet this valley will be filled with water, and you, your cattle and your other animals will drink. This is an easy thing in the eyes of the Lord; he will also hand Moab over to you. (2 Kings 3:16-18)

God gave Joram's team a part in solving their problem. Their part was digging ditches, which is hard, unromantic work. But they were party to a miracle. The water came, and Moab was defeated.

Mothering is like ditch-digging. As mothers we can do nothing to persuade or convince our children to love God. We can dig the ditches, but we can't fill them. We can teach our children about God, pray for them, live the Christian life before them, and expose them to others who love and serve God. But only God can give them spiritual life. God doesn't need our help, but in His sovereign plan He invites us to take part actively—to colabor with Him as He works in their lives.

The story is told of a frightened girl who calls her mother repeatedly to her bedside. Her exasperated mother says, "Sweetheart, Mommie told you already you don't need to be frightened; God is with you."

"I know," the little girl replied, "but I need somebody here with skin on."

One of the times when we can demonstrate our part in child raising is when our children are frightened. When fear crouches at the foot of my child's bed, I use the situation to point him to God. I provide the skin. I dig the ditches.

These are some of the ditches I dig to help my children overcome fear:

♦ Sometimes I sit by their beds and sing hymns for a while, or sit outside their doors in the hallway and read Scripture. I often choose an appropriate verse or short passage on courage and trusting God to read aloud several times, so they can grasp and hold fast God's words to them.

♦ I tell Bible stories that demonstrate God's faithfulness in helping and protecting His people. I may ask, "Who are some people in the Bible who faced scary situations?" The answers would include Daniel in the lions' den, Paul on board ship in a storm, David facing Goliath, or the people of Israel trapped between the Red Sea and the rapidly approaching Egyptian army. Then we recall the outcome and how God helped them. This stirs the child to trust God in his situation.

♦ I tell stories of God's protection and care in our own family and in the lives of other believers. Missionary biographies and newsletters often provide incidents ranging from the dramatic to the commonplace that vividly illustrate God's involvement and care.

In times of fear or indecision, people are often especially responsive to God's Word. The psalmist wrote, "It was good for me to be afflicted so that I might learn your decrees" (Psalm 119:71). Hard times often provide fertile opportunities for Bible memorization and meditation. Isaiah 41:10 and Psalm 34:7 are appropriate verses for a frightened child to memorize.

After a time of closeness during a frightening experience, I gradually increase my distance away from them and encourage them to trust God. It may mean moving into the hallway, or saying, "I need to check on the coffee cake I'm baking for breakfast" or, "I'll check in on you after I fold a batch of clothes."

The object is to "put the skin on" their learning about God. As they personally experience God's help and His answers to their prayers, and as they realize the reliability of the Bible, God will be more real and personal to them.

C. S. Lewis in *The Efficacy of Prayer* further develops this thought about the part we play in God's work.

> He could, if He chose, repair our bodies miraculously without food; or give us food without the aid of farmers, bakers, and butchers; or knowledge without the aid of learned men; or convert the heathen without missionaries. Instead, He allows soil and weather and animals, and the muscles, minds and wills of men to co-operate in the execution of His will.[2]

Exercising our muscles, mind, and will is our part.

We put the skin on God's plan for our children. We pray for them and with them concerning their fears; we teach them the importance of honesty despite widespread cheating; we train them to obey, and teach them how to show respect for parents and other adults. We love, encourage, and build them up with words, hugs, and looks of love and acceptance. Our part is reading them Bible stories, helping them learn spelling and fractions, reminding them to practice the piano, and driving them to the dentist. In all these things we must be fully aware that unless God builds the house our labor is in vain—while also remembering that every wise woman builds her house. We cannot work without God's help, and He invites us to cooperate with Him in the building process.

QUESTIONS FOR REFLECTION OR DISCUSSION

1. In what ways are you growing in your understanding that your child is from God and for His purposes?
2. In 2 Kings 3:16-20 the armies dug ditches and God sent water to fill them. The more ditches they dug the more water could be captured for their use. List five ditches you might dig in your children's lives.
3. Our part is "our very best mothering—done in faith." What does that mean to you?
4. What are the things only God can do in our children's lives?

NOTES
   1. As quoted by J. C. Ryle in *Christian Leaders of the Eighteenth Century* (Banner of Truth Trust, 1978), p. 297.
   2. C. S. Lewis, *The Efficacy of Prayer* (Harcourt, Brace and World, 1960), pp. 8-9.

Chapter Six

GETTING IN STEP
WITH GOD

"I can't believe they're all from the same family." Mrs. Anibal, a pert, blonde woman who taught kindergarten to all three Flemings, verbalized what I often felt. Three children. Same parents. Same environment. Same genes. How can they be so different?

Observing our children's differences convinces me that God loves diversity. He is the God of the individual. No two children are entirely alike—not even twins.

After testing hundreds of newborns at the Albert Einstein College of Medicine, psychiatrist Wagner H. Bridger concluded that before his environment shaped him, your child was already a unique individual. He arrived with a basic makeup that will determine how he relates to life outside the womb. His study convinced him that "infants show stable temperamental differences right at birth."[1]

Newborns arrive with temperaments that even influence how they approach their first task—eating. Some infants fall asleep during feedings, and some appear to be daydreaming and many need encouragement to finish a meal. Others stick with the job methodically until the breast or bottle is empty. Others attack their meals like barracudas. I am not suggesting you "type" your baby by his first feeding, but that you recognize he possesses individual characteristics when you welcome him into the world.

"Ramona is so tidy she embarrasses me," moaned her mother, Alice. Ramona is a fastidious two-year-old. When other children come to play, Ramona frustrates them by putting toys away while they are trying to play with them. Her tidiness became a real problem when Grandma came to visit. Ramona whisked the ashtray off the table and ran to empty it each time Granny put in a few ashes.

Alice and her husband Larry were neat, but generally relaxed about maintaining their home and in their overall approach to life. "Where did Ramona get her fetish for neatness?" they asked. "Certainly not from us."

Ramona was born an individual—one with a tidy, orderly makeup. She did not learn her preoccupation with cleanliness from her parents; there was something inherently present in her personality from birth.

My mother would have gladly swapped me for a Ramona because I had a pronounced bent too—not toward neatness, but quite the opposite. As a little girl I loved horses and drew pictures of them constantly. Mom put her foot down after I had accumulated three boxes of horse drawings under my bed. She told me to eliminate two boxes. So I began the tedious but sentimental project of sorting through my beloved horses.

This wasn't merely a matter of shuffling paper. Each horse was named and had peculiar characteristics. I sorted them into "most loved," "second most loved," and "loved" piles on my bed. I was emotionally drained by trying to decide which ones to part with. After an hour or so of work I took a break.

When I next returned to my room it was bedtime, and I had forgotten my project. There it was, half done, looming up like a mountain on my bed. Without blinking an eye, I changed into my pajamas, shook the covers, and climbed into bed while the fluttering papers settled to the floor all around my bed. I was not, and still am not, a Ramona.

Training can modify or develop a child's natural bent, but we must realize she is not a blank paper on which we sketch her full personality and destiny. She came to us already an individual—a person without language, experience, or maturity, but still a person.

Dr. Bridger's findings about the individuality of babies come as no surprise to people who study the Bible. In Psalm 139 we discover the reason why children are born as individuals. In this prayer to God, David wrote,

> For you created my inmost being; you knit me together in my mother's womb. I praise you because I am fearfully and wonderfully made; your works are wonderful, I know that full well. My frame was not hidden from you when I was made in the secret place. When I was woven together in the depths of the earth, your eyes saw my unformed body. All the days ordained for me were written in your book before one of them came to be. (Psalm 139:13-16)

God focuses His attention on the individual. He does not produce babies by mass production, nor are they developed by accident or chance. Rather, God Himself forms each child one by one.

Because God handcrafts our children individually, they are all different. God designed each child as a unique person.

LORD, WHY?

We may wish God would form them more to our specifications, or at least consult with us about our preferences. But He doesn't. Tempted to complain, we may ask:

"Lord, couldn't You have given Emily a higher IQ?"

"Why didn't You make Sidney more athletic?"

"Couldn't You have made Allison more graceful, Lord?"

"Lord, why did You have to stick Charlie with such big ears?"

But to complaints such as these, God replies, "Do you question me about my children, or give me orders about the work of my hands?" (Isaiah 45:11).

CREATED FOR GOD'S GLORY

Often the next question that bolts wildly from our lips is "Why?" Why did God make my little child with these shortcomings? The answer is often far deeper than our minds can fathom, but in simple form we find it in Isaiah 43:7, where God speaks of His sons and daughters *"whom I created for my glory."*

Created for His glory—what a staggering thought! God formed each of us for His glory. But what does that mean?

The Hebrew word for *glory* used in Isaiah 43:7 is the same word used to describe a man's wealth, splendor, or reputation. We find this word also in Exodus 33 when Moses asks God, "Show me your glory." God drew back the curtains of heaven and allowed Moses to view His goodness, His mercy, His compassion, and His holiness. He allowed Moses to catch a glimpse of the wonder of God.

Later, even pagan nations heard of the Israelites'

miraculous deliverance from Egypt, and a "great fear" fell on them. Rahab, a pagan prostitute, had reverence for God because of the awesome ways in which He worked for His people. "The Lord your God is God in heaven above and on the earth below," she declared in Joshua 2:11. Through events that showed His glory, God revealed Himself in ways people could understand.

You may be asking, "I understand that God shows Himself as God when he holds back the Red Sea or turns the Nile to blood, but how does he show Himself as God through my little Herbie?"

First, Herbie is "fearfully and wonderfully made." Remember the first time you saw Herbie? It didn't matter to you that he was red, wrinkled, and bald. You gazed at him with a sense of wonder. He was so small, yet so perfect. You opened his tiny fist to inspect his fingers, and uncovered his feet to count his toes. The closer you looked, the more convinced you were that you had given birth to a miracle.

Second, God created Herbie with a unique personality because He has a special purpose in mind for him. Herbie was not mass-produced and randomly assigned a meaningless purpose. Herbie's individuality and life's purpose are closely linked. God wove and knit Herbie together to fit His plans for him.

I like to imagine what various Bible characters were like as children. Was Samson a ninety-pound weakling as a boy? Was Jeremiah a hardhearted child, transformed only later into a tenderhearted, weeping prophet?

I don't think so. They didn't suddenly become strong, compassionate, or bold as they began their ministries. I believe God used their natural personalities, as well as times of special preparation and training, to fit them for their work. I think the same basic makeup characterized these Bible heroes in both childhood and adulthood. Certain characteristics were wrought into their being in the womb.

Your Herbie is God's creation too, and his personality was custom-made for a purpose. God has plans for Herbie.

A Unique Plan for Each Child

Sometimes God lets parents in on his plans for their children.

A childless couple, Manoah and his wife lived in the hill country of Zorah around 1090 B.C. An angel appeared to Manoah's wife and promised her a son and described God's plan for the child's life.

> You are sterile and childless, but you are going to conceive and have a son. Now see to it that you drink no wine or other fermented drink and that you do not eat anything unclean, because you will conceive and give birth to a son. No razor may be used on his head, because the boy is to be a Nazirite, set apart to God from birth, and he will begin the deliverance of Israel from the hands of the Philistines. (Judges 13:3-5)

The child was Samson. More than a thousand years later, just prior to the birth of Christ, another childless couple received similar good news: God planned to give them a son also. Once again, an angel shared God's plan for the unconceived child's life.

> Do not be afraid, Zechariah; your prayer has been heard. Your wife Elizabeth will bear you a son, and you are to give him the name John. He will be a joy and delight to you, and many will rejoice because

of his birth, for he will be great in the sight of the
Lord. He is never to take wine or other fermented
drink, and he will be filled with the Holy Spirit
even from birth. Many of the people of Israel will
he bring back to the Lord their God. And he will
go on before the Lord, in the spirit and power of
Elijah, to turn the hearts of the fathers to their
children and the disobedient to the wisdom of the
righteous—to make ready a people prepared for
the Lord. (Luke 1:13-17)

Zechariah and Elizabeth's son John became a bold,
fiercely independent preacher who prepared the way for
Christ.

Obviously, God rarely reveals His plans to parents
today by having angels visit us. But God still has plans in
mind for our children, just as He did for Jeremiah:
"Before I formed you in the womb I knew you, before
you were born I set you apart; I appointed you as a
prophet to the nations" (Jeremiah 1:5).

While I was expecting Matthew, Roger and I were
impressed that the verses given to Zechariah regarding
the birth of John the Baptist had relevance to our
unborn child. Perhaps the significance of the verses is
no more than "he will be a joy and delight to you, and
many will rejoice because of his birth." That much has
already happened! But God may have in mind to one
day make him "great in the sight of the Lord," or to
use him to bring people "back to the Lord their God,"
or to "turn the hearts of the fathers to their children."
We don't know what God has in mind, but we believe
that God has plans for him, and for his sister, Beth,
and brother, Graham, and for each of your children as
well.

STRENGTHS AND WEAKNESSES

Part of God's plan is to show Himself in and through your child's strengths and weaknesses. Often these strengths and weaknesses are closely intertwined, as illustrated by this conversation between Becky's mother and a neighbor:

> MOTHER: Becky has a strong, confident personality.
> NEIGHBOR: That's good!
> MOTHER: Not always, because she is also very strong-willed.
> NEIGHBOR: That's too bad!
> MOTHER: No, that's good because she isn't easily swayed by peer pressure.
> NEIGHBOR: That's good!
> MOTHER: Well, not always, because she isn't easily swayed by me either.
> NEIGHBOR: That's too bad!
> MOTHER: But Becky is very capable and independent. She learned to dress and feed herself when she was very young.
> NEIGHBOR: That's good!
> MOTHER: Yes, but she is easily frustrated if she can't perform on the same level as her older brothers and sisters. Sometimes she gives way to temper.
> NEIGHBOR: That's too bad!
> MOTHER: Yes, but. . . .

Our children's strengths and weaknesses are intertwined. The same characteristics may have both positive and negative aspects, and a change of viewpoint can change strengths into weaknesses or weaknesses into strengths. Laura often tried to motivate her carefree daughter Cindy to give more attention to her appearance by citing her friend Victoria as an example of good grooming. Victoria was a strikingly pretty eleven-year-old, always impeccably groomed, every hair in place, with spotless clothes, matching socks, ribbons, and barrettes. Then one day Victoria came to spend a weekend with Cindy's family. After dinner the first night they all decided to go out for ice cream. Victoria disappeared "to change into something more appropriate." The family waited and waited. Victoria put on a new outfit, combed and brushed her hair, readjusted her clothes, and finally emerged ready for ice cream. Laura discovered that every activity required a "more appropriate" outfit and Victoria changed frequently every day. As Laura waited she watched the laundry stack grow while Victoria went from outfit to outfit. Her admiration for Victoria turned to disdain. Harsh words such as *vain, self-centered,* and *egotistical* replaced *charming, impeccable,* and *well-groomed* in Laura's descriptions of Victoria. Victoria hadn't changed, but Laura's insight into Victoria had altered dramatically. Laura also came to better appreciate Cindy's punctuality and her sensible, relaxed attitude about her appearance.

Every strength has a corresponding weakness. A creative child may also be a daydreamer. The child with zest and enthusiasm may also slam doors and talk too loudly.

For every weakness you identify in your child, try to pinpoint corresponding strengths. Focus on the positive possibilities, and help your child recognize and develop his potential.

The weaknesses themselves may be the vehicles God uses to bring glory to His name. Weaknesses often heighten your child's consciousness of his need for God and provide natural opportunities for him to experience God's help. The ability to view areas of weakness with the confidence that God wants to reveal Himself in your child's life will alleviate anxiety and promote faith in both you and your child.

In her book *The Hearing Heart,* Hannah Hurnard related an incident that illustrates God's ability to reveal Himself to us through our weaknesses.

All her life Hannah Hurnard had stammered severely and been painfully shy. Even mustering up enough courage as a new Christian to start Bible school was a glowing tribute to God's grace at work in her life. Hannah loved Christ. She relished her times alone with Him every day—time spent reading her Bible and praying. In these times God deeply impressed 2 Corinthians 12:9 on her mind: "But he said to me, 'My grace is sufficient for you, for my power is made perfect in weakness.' Therefore I will boast all the more gladly about my weaknesses, so that Christ's power may rest on me."

Soon afterward, God gave Hannah an opportunity to experience the reality of this promise. Imagine the anxiety an average person feels when asked to make a speech. Now magnify the terror ten times for a shy, stuttering girl who could scarcely tell a train conductor her destination.

As the day for the speech approached, every fiber of Hannah's being wanted to bound away, to escape from her intense, overpowering fear. But God brought Hannah face to face with His promise. The issue became, "Will you believe Me for 2 Corinthians 12:9? Will you trust Me that your weakness is an opportunity for Me to reveal Myself in your life?"

Hannah spoke on 2 Corinthians 12:9 and gave her entire talk without a stammer. That day God showed Himself to Hannah and her classmates.

God could have removed Hannah's speech impediment totally and permanently. He never did. It was His gift to Hannah. Her weakness constantly reminded her to trust God. It was a vehicle through which He revealed Himself as God.

But how does this relate to mothers?

PRAYER AND PLANNING FOR MOTHERS

Pause for a moment and visualize each of your children. Bring them one at a time before God in prayer. Use these thoughts to help you pray:

> *Acknowledge* that God's hand was on your child in the way he or she was formed before birth, according to God's good plan.
>
> *Admit* any areas you resent in the way God put your child together.
>
> *Accept* God's design for your child. Thank God for making your child the way he is.
>
> *Affirm* God's purpose in creating your child for His glory.
>
> *Ally* yourself with God in His plans for your child's life.

The goal of parenting is not for us to decide what we want our children to become and then ruthlessly teach, train, squeeze, badger, and cajole them into that mold. Instead, we must recognize that God has already designed them. God already has a mature person and a long-range purpose in mind. Our job is to see our children as God does—and to involve ourselves in God's plans for them. Like a sculptor, we must try to see the final form straining to break out of the uncut stone.

This cannot be accomplished without prayer and planning. But when we most need it, we seem to have so little time left in which to pray and plan.

When we were missionaries in Okinawa our children

included a three-year-old, a two-year-old, and an infant. In those days I considered brushing my teeth recreation. Free time was nonexistent. I never had time for everything I felt I should do, let alone the things I wanted to do.

Usually, extra people lived with us for training in Christian discipleship. Bible studies and meetings were often held in our home. Our ministry to servicemen often included cooking for large numbers. This relentless pressure forced me to decide what to do and what to leave undone.

Jesus faced the same time crunch. But He nevertheless took time for prayer and planning. We see a description of His action-packed ministry in Mark 1:29-39.

The word must have leaked out after Jesus healed Simon's mother-in-law, because at sunset "the whole town gathered at the door, and Jesus healed many who had various diseases." It must have been a very busy night, but early the following morning, "while it was still dark, Jesus got up, left the house and went off to a solitary place, where he prayed."

All too soon, I'm sure, Jesus' quiet prayer retreat was shattered by His disciples. "Simon and his companions went to look for him, and when they found him they exclaimed: 'Everyone is looking for you!' " A responsive crowd, large numbers clamoring for His attention—what a wonderful, exciting opportunity for further ministry. But wait! Jesus replied, "Let us go somewhere else—to the nearby villages—so I can preach there also. That is why I have come."

Why leave a golden opportunity? Because Jesus was in step with His Father. They had just spent face-to-face time together in prayer in that solitary place. Jesus had taken time to get God's strategy for His ministry. Shouldn't we follow His example? Can we neglect the priority and necessity of spending time in prayer and planning?

Time spent in prayer and planning helps us see our children as God does. Prayer and planning aligns us with His purposes for them. Children cannot be put on hold, or laid aside like a wallpaper project, for our convenience. They can't wait for our day off, or for the day when we finally have everything under control! God has given us the privilege of working together with Him on behalf of our children, and they must be a priority.

Taking this time alone refreshes and clarifies my commitment to the mothering assignment God has given me. I use prayer and planning time to evaluate myself: "Lord, am I doing what You want me to do?"

Time for prayer also reminds me that I colabor with God. I am not in this alone.

Fresh insights about my children and a new perspective on mothering often come to me during time in prayer. This is how I gain new understanding and practical ideas for building my home.

Time for prayer and planning also gives me an opportunity to think carefully about each child individually. This deepens my appreciation of that child and helps me know how to pray for that child. Praying, thinking, and jotting down observations helps me see needs that could otherwise go unnoticed and unattended.

When I did this recently, I remembered that each of my children had been asking to spend some time alone with me. All three requested this more than once in the last couple of weeks. "What does this mean?" I asked. "How can I get in step with God about this?"

We had just returned from a few days of vacation, so our schedule wasn't too busy. Even during our vacation Beth and Graham had both asked me to take walks alone with them. They each needed time with me to talk, time when they knew they would have my undivided attention. Many things were on their minds: school started soon, a friend was being buffeted by his parents' divorce, and each one was at a unique stage in personal development. Time spent praying and listening to God regarding my children helped me identify this area of need. As well as praying carefully, I could plan specific ways for each child to get adequate time alone with me.

When her son Philip was eighteen months old, Linda began wondering how this child could be hers. Could she have brought the wrong baby home from the hospital? He didn't look like either her or her husband, and didn't act like them either. Philip was stubborn and hot-tempered. *If he is this difficult at eighteen months, she thought, what will he be like at eighteen years?*

Linda dreaded certain everyday activities like dressing Philip. He insisted on doing everything himself—even putting on his own shoes and tying them. But his coordination lagged behind his determination. His little fingers could not put on his shoes, let alone tie them. Philip often vented his frustration with an explosion of rage.

One day after Linda and her husband spent time praying together about this, her husband commented, "I think Philip is frustrated. He isn't trying to exasperate us. He sees the older children dressing themselves and he wants to do what they do. I've watched him play. He attempts to do whatever the other children do and then gets frustrated because he can't keep up. Philip doesn't realize he has limitations simply because he is younger. I see some very fine qualities in Philip. He has drive and ambition. It's wonderful that he tries to do these things for himself."

Linda began to realize her irritated response to Philip did not help. She tried to understand his frustrations. If I were Philip, she asked herself, how would I want my mother to treat me? Linda remembered frustrating incidents in her own life when she attempted something but performed poorly. She remembered God's patience, understanding, and help in those times.

So the next time Philip struggled with his shoes, Linda stepped in quickly and said, "Philip, I'm so proud of you for trying to put on your shoes. You are quite a boy! Soon you'll be able to do this all by yourself. But your fingers aren't quite ready yet. Would you like me to help you get them on?"

Perhaps it was the tone of Linda's voice, or her facial expression, but Philip seemed to grasp what she was saying. It was a turning point in their relationship.

Linda and her husband continued to work on Philip's temper, but the insight God gave them following their prayer time had changed their family. This prayer time was the key that unlocked a disturbing situation. And Linda is now convinced that Philip really is her son. He looks more and more like his father, and Linda suspects that his stubbornness and temper were inherited after all.

Philip's strengths are becoming more obvious too. He exudes enthusiasm and a zest for life. He remains determined, eager, and adventurous. But his frustration has lessened, now that his body can keep up.

When we take time to pray and think carefully about each of our children, God allows us to see the positive in the negative, the answer in the confusion, and the encouraging in the discouraging.

How to Take a Spiritual Inventory of Your Child

1. Set aside some time to be alone with God. Perhaps your husband will watch your children one Saturday to let you get a few hours alone with the Lord. Or you might be able to trade baby-sitting with another mother.

2. Consider spending a large block of time in prayer. There are many excellent ways to use your time profitably, whether you are spending two hours or a full day alone with God.

3. Spend your time reading God's Word, looking for God's directions, and praying. Your goal is to get in step with God and His plans for you and your children not merely thinking your own thoughts.

4. I usually reserve the last hour of my time alone to think about and pray for each of my children individually. Put each child's name at the top of a separate sheet of paper and jot down all the ideas that come to mind about that child. Here's an example of a completed inventory.

Strengths
1. Faithful, makes his bed every morning without being reminded.
2. Artist / creative.
3. Gentle and sensitive (kind to younger children and people who are hurting).
4. Strong sense of right and wrong.

Weaknesses
1. Disorganized—forgetful (forgot lunch three times this week).
2. Ungrateful (always asks in prayer, rarely thanks).

Observations
1. More conscious of physical appearance recently (grooming, clothes).
2. Giggly—gets into giggling seizures with brother.
3. Apprehensive about school—maybe this is why he forgets his lunch.
4. Likes dogs.

Application
1. To help Herbie be more organized in the morning, I will have him put all his school things together by the front door before coming to breakfast. I'll explain why I think this will help him.
2. I will pray with him each morning before he leaves for school, focusing his attention on God as his caring Father, and seeking to ease his apprehension about school.
3. Pray and ask God to help me identify the root of his anxiety about school.

STRENGTHS

When I evaluate my children in this way, I list several strengths. Always list more strengths than weaknesses. Your focus should be on the positive.

Try to think broadly about each child, considering him spiritually, physically, socially, intellectually, and emotionally. Pay close attention to emerging character traits.

Keep current. Human beings are dynamic, not static. Your child is not the same today as he was yesterday. His personality changes and deepens. His interests diversify. He is constantly becoming a new person.

WEAKNESSES

Weaknesses are a real blessing. Navigator staff member Jim White wrote, "One of the devil's key strategies is to convince a Christian that God has no future for failures. The truth of the matter is, failure is sometimes the very experience that enables God to later use us and still get all the glory."

Properly viewed, weaknesses can be wonderful. And time alone with God gives the best possible vantage point for viewing them. Prayer and planning time gives us God's perspective on weakness, failure, and current problems. It may seem a life-or-death issue to a fourth grader that he struck out three times in the baseball game, but it will mean little when he is forty. We can sympathize with him and help him accept personal failure as a constructive experience. We can remind him that all truly great men experience failure.

This perspective enables us to sympathize and encourage. We might say, "Sammy, I understand how you feel about striking out. Everyone experiences times of failure. A man named Harry Truman, for example, was not able to play sports. He spent much of his free time reading—especially history. Later he became our president, and it was good that he knew history better than baseball."

When a child faces failure or trials, remember that his life will cover many years. His life won't end if he loses a game, fails a course, or is hurt by a close friend.

Viewing our children's weaknesses through the perspective of a lifetime can ease our concern about certain problems, but make others seem more serious. For example, dishonesty or laziness should be deliberately confronted because of their disastrous effects over a lifetime.

OBSERVATIONS

I like to regularly list observations for each child. This practice gives me insight into their personalities and develops me as a better "child-watcher."

Jane Goodall, a British scientist, spent much of her life in Africa observing chimpanzees. She painstakingly invested hundreds of hours watching them, and collected and compiled data based on her careful study. As

I read the *National Geographic* article describing her work, I thought, *I wonder if Jane Goodall knows her monkeys better than I know mine?* We can ask God's help to become better students of our children.

APPLICATION

The next step is determining something I can do to help my child continue to develop into the person God wants him to become. Choose one area from your inventory— a strength to enhance, or a weakness to overcome.

Management consultants tell business executives not to pour energy and time into helping people with their weaknesses, but to engage them in opportunities to maximize their strengths. Mothers, too, can profit from this principle.

If a child excels in creative writing but is poor in math, do not focus *solely* on his weakness in math. Explore possibilities for developing his writing ability— let him write the family's Christmas newsletter, or encourage him to enter a young writer's contest.

If your child is a faithful bed maker, for example, you could encourage this strength by leaving notes on his pillow or in his lunch box, thanking him for making his bed. Or, you could express appreciation and give him another responsibility (cutting grass, or washing the car), with recognition: "Dad and I decided to give you this responsibility because we know we can count on you."

If your child is artistic, provide opportunities for him to try new art projects: sponge painting, crayon, collage. Or, visit an art museum.

If you want your child to be more thankful, during prayer time together you could make a list of things your family has to be thankful for. Ask him to choose a few items and thank God for them in prayer.

PRAYER

Our prayer and planning times help us see each child more clearly. While your thoughts are fresh, jot down some specific things to pray for your child. And keep your prayer lists where you can use them often—in your Bible, beside your bed, or on the refrigerator.

God chose your family as the best environment for your child's development. He chose you as his mother. God has plans for your child, and you can be His partner through prayer and planning.

Taking a regular spiritual inventory of each child can help you avoid the tendency to get into a rut and "think yesterday's thoughts" about them. A child who did several irresponsible things six months ago may not have done anything irresponsible recently. Don't nail him forever in a box labeled "irresponsible." Ask God to help you view your child fairly and freshly every day.

QUESTIONS FOR REFLECTION OR DISCUSSION

1. What is the most delightful thing about your child?
2. Choose three words that describe your child.
3. Pray through the section of this chapter titled *Prayer and Planning for Mothers* to Acknowledge, Admit, Accept, Affirm, and Ally yourself with God. What did you learn about yourself from this exercise?
4. Do a Spiritual Inventory on your child.

NOTE
   1. Julius Segal and Herbert Yahraes, "Bringing Up Mother," *Psychology Today,* November 1978, p. 90.

Chapter Seven

GOING BEYOND "GOD BLESS CHARLIE"

If Jesus Christ faced you squarely with the question, "What is it you want?"—what would you ask Him to do for you?

Then think of your children. What would you want Jesus to do for each of them? What requests should you make for them? Are there any guidelines to help you know what to pray? How can you get beyond simply, "God bless Charlie"?

Grappling with these questions forces us to examine our glib, quick, conscience-easer prayers and to rethink our motives and the content of our prayers for our children.

Jesus faced another mother with a similar question many years ago. She was the wife of Zebedee, and was the mother of James and John, two of Jesus' disciples. I like to refer to her, affectionately, as Mrs. Z. Let's look at Mrs. Z's encounter with the Lord in Matthew 20:20-28.

Jesus' followers were thinking of kings and kingdoms. As He moved toward Jerusalem, their expectations of future greatness rose steadily. With high hopes, Mrs. Z and her sons followed in the wake of the popular mood.

Mrs. Z saw that her sons enjoyed a favored position with Jesus. Often when He withdrew from the crowds, He took James and John with Him. So now she approached Jesus to make her appeal. As she knelt before him, Jesus focused His attention on her and asked, "What is it you want?"

AN ASTOUNDING REQUEST

Mrs. Z knew what she wanted. Her request was ready. She stated it simply and concisely. "Grant that one of these two sons of mine may sit at your right and the other at your left in your kingdom."

What an astounding request! What more could you ask of a king than to be ranked second and third in His kingdom? This woman either possessed tremendous courage and vision, or tremendous gall.

Jesus gave her no assurance that He would ever fulfill her request, but said, "You don't know what you are asking." His Father alone would decide who would sit on His left and right in the kingdom. Only time will tell if she received her request, but Jesus promised her nothing.

When the other disciples heard about this request, they became highly indignant about such an attempted power grab. What right did James and John have to receive a more prominent position than the others? Even though most Bible teachers today give this woman scant praise, I find plenty here to challenge my thinking about prayer.

This woman made time to approach Jesus—to kneel and to ask. We too must make time for prayer. In *Quiet Talks on Prayer,* S.D. Gordon observes,

> The great people of earth are the people who pray.
> I do not mean those who talk about prayer; nor
> those who say they believe in prayer; nor yet those

who can explain about prayer; but I mean those people who *take time and pray.* They have not time. It must be taken from something else. This something else is important—very important, and pressing, but still less important and pressing than prayer.[1]

Unless I schedule time for serious prayer, my hours evaporate and I neglect it. Each morning I try to set aside time to read my Bible and pray. Whether long and reflective or brief and compact, my quiet time alone with God only happens consistently when I make it a priority. Only my commitment keeps the pressures and activities of life from squeezing this appointment with God out of my schedule.

My prayer times can expand if I develop the habit of praying in the midst of other activities. I can pray as I walk through our neighborhood, wash the dishes, stir the oatmeal, or walk to the car. When I eat lunch alone I pray for my children. Currently I'm trying to remember to pray for each family member as we eat dinner.

When our children were small, my times spent apart in uninterrupted prayer were brief. But I found I could stretch my total prayer time if I allowed routine tasks to trigger prayer. Even though they're older now, I still follow this practice.

As I feed the children, I pray God will nourish their souls; as I bathe them I pray they will experience the spiritual cleansing Christ provides; as I dress them I pray they will be clothed in righteousness.

Time to intercede for our children may seem scarce, but if we plan at least a brief time to pray each day, and combine prayer with routine activities, we may greatly increase the prayer we invest in our children's behalf. We must make and take time to pray.

SHE KNEW WHAT SHE WANTED

When Jesus asked Mrs. Z what she wanted, she didn't hesitate. Obviously, she had already thought about her request.

Planning ahead, for me, usually results in a list. I make do-lists, grocery lists, and correspondence lists. My daily destiny is often closely linked to a handwritten, often jelly-splattered list. If I lose my list, the day is shot. The same is true of my praying. Without an updated list, my prayer life crumbles.

A list helps me avoid a rambling, haphazard, hit-or-miss approach to prayer. It forces me to clarify and specify what I want God to do for our children.

Roger writes prayer items on index cards. He keeps a card for each family member, listing his requests and recording answers when they come. Reviewing how God works increases his faith, and provides specific material for praising God.

Think carefully about your prayers for your children. Decide what you should ask Jesus to do for each of them, consider writing down your requests, and keep a record of God's answers.

SHE ASKED BIG

However defective her theology, Mrs. Z knew that Jesus would soon be king, so she acted to ensure that her sons would have two of the key positions in the kingdom. Even if her motives were questionable, we can learn something about asking God to do something big for our children from her example.

But what is a *big* prayer request? Should we pray that our children will be healthy, wealthy, and wise? Should we pray that they would pastor a large church, found a foreign mission, or speak for Christ before millions? Are any of these requests big in God's eyes?

Jesus said, "Whoever wants to become great among you must be your servant, and whoever wants to be first must be your slave—just as the Son of Man did not come to be served, but to serve, and to give his life as a ransom for many" (Matthew 20:26-28). If we want our children to be great, we must first pray that they become servants.

Confused goals and twisted values can distort our prayers. What seems good to us may not necessarily be good in God's eyes.

A young Englishman named Forbes Robinson recognized long ago his own imperfect concept of God, and prayed prayers bigger than his limited understanding. In a letter to a friend, Robinson wrote:

> I want you to be one of the best men that ever lived—to see God and to reveal him to men. This is the burden of my prayers. My whole being goes out in passionate entreaty to God that he will give me what I ask. I am sure he will, for the request is after his own heart.
>
> I do not pray that you may succeed in life, or "get on" in this world. I seldom ever pray that you may love me better, or that I may see you oftener in this or any other world—much as I crave this.
>
> But I ask, I implore, that Christ may be formed in you, that you may be made not in any likeness suggested by my imagination, but in the image of God—that you may realize not my, but his ideal—however much that ideal may bewilder me, however little I may recognize it when it is created.
>
> I hate the thought that out of love for me you should accept my presentation, my feeble ideal, of the Christ. I want God to reveal his Son to you independently of men—to give you a first-hand

knowledge of him whom I am only beginning to see.
Sometimes more selfish thoughts will intrude, but this represents the main current of my prayers. And if this is to be won from heaven by importunity, by ceaseless begging, I think I shall get it for you![2]

We may conclude that the mother of James and John asked for the wrong thing for the wrong reason. She was position-oriented and status-conscious when she made her request.

But if she asked improperly, what is a valid prayer request? As I try to discern what God wants me to pray for my children, several guidelines help me check my motives and gauge whether my prayers are for God's glory or my own. As you seek to "ask big," these guidelines may be helpful:

1. Pray for them to *have a place in the kingdom*—pray for each child's salvation.
2. Pray that they would *be a credit to the kingdom*— that each child will develop a godly character.
3. Pray that they would *be used to promote the kingdom*— that each child will become a servant of others.

A Place in the Kingdom

Our first consideration is for our children's salvation. If they are to have a place in the kingdom of God, they must personally come to Christ and experience the new birth.

Monica, the devout mother of Saint Augustine, prayed fervently for her son's salvation. But Augustine's nonChristian father was as zealous to lead Augustine into sin as Monica was to introduce him to Christ—and Augustine showed little spiritual interest.

One day Monica approached a bishop who was known for his knowledge of the Scriptures and his habit of talking to people about their need for salvation. She asked him to speak to Augustine, but the bishop refused. Finally, as Monica became more earnest in her appeals, the exasperated bishop reportedly exclaimed, "It cannot be that the son of these tears should perish."

After he became a Christian, Augustine wrote in prayer of his indebtedness to his mother's intercession: "And now didst thou 'stretch forth thy hand from above' and didst draw up my soul out of that profound darkness because my mother, thy faithful one, wept to thee on my behalf more than mothers are accustomed to weep for the bodily deaths of their children."[3]

Many centuries later, on a Saturday afternoon in 1849, another mother prayed for the salvation of her only son, Hudson Taylor.

"Leaving her friends she went alone to plead with God for his salvation. Hour after hour passed while that mother was still upon her knees, until her heart was flooded with a joyful assurance that her prayers were heard and answered."[4]

When Mrs. Taylor returned home, her son told her of his conversion. Hudson Taylor later founded the China Inland Mission. He ministered to countless Chinese, and his example has inspired thousands of missionaries. His life still speaks today to those who have been deeply challenged by his devotion to Christ.

Another mother I know, the wife of the leader of a Christian organization, sets an example to mothers by her perseverance in prayer. Several of her children have slipped in and out of fellowship with God over the years, but their mother keeps praying, tirelessly. Their growth in grace must be largely the result of her prayers.

Even when it seems God does not hear our prayers for our children, we must keep on praying persistently. Prayer may be our most effective ministry in our children's lives. It is never too early to begin praying for our children's salvation. We even prayed for our children before they were conceived.

On our wedding day, Roger and I knelt beside our bed to commit our marriage to God, to read several psalms, and to pray. God gave us an unexpected wedding present during our first devotional time as husband and wife. He impressed on us a verse—Psalm 147:13—promising his blessing on our children. After we thanked God, Roger wrote, "God's Wedding Gift 7/31/65" beside that verse in our Bibles.

Throughout our marriage we have reviewed that encouraging word from God again and again. God's promise to "bless our children within us" reassured us that we were waiting for a particular baby—one blessed by God. And we prayed this child would know God's salvation.

From the first fluttering movement to later side-jarring kicks, we prayed throughout the pregnancy for this baby's eventual salvation. Finally, we had the joy of seeing Matthew, our new son. Holding him in our arms, we prayed that he would have a place in the kingdom. Night after night, as we laid our infant in his crib, we prayed for him. As the years passed, our prayers continued.

One night in his upper bunk, he prayed and gave his life to Jesus. The Holy Spirit entered his life, and a new spiritual life began. He had a place in the kingdom.

We prayed for a place in the kingdom for each of our children, and now we pray for our children's children too. It is impossible to begin too soon, or to pray too much for our children.

Going Beyond "God Bless Charlie"

A CREDIT TO THE KINGDOM

If our first prayer must be for our children's salvation, our second must be for their character. They must gradually mature, becoming more and more like Christ.

Jesus Christ is our King and we are His subjects. Christ's goal for His subjects is the development of Christlike character and conduct. God wants His kingdom to be inhabited by a changed people, people whose characters are like His.

> For the grace of God that brings salvation has appeared to all men. It teaches us to say "No" to ungodliness and worldly passions, and to live self controlled, upright and godly lives in this present age, while we wait for the blessed hope—the glorious appearing of our great God and Savior, Jesus Christ, who gave himself for us to redeem us from all wickedness and to purify for himself a people that are his very own, eager to do what is good. (Titus 2:11-14)

Hannah is another example of a mother who helped make her son a credit to God's kingdom through prayer. Painful years of waiting to conceive a child had already taken their toll when we first meet Hannah in the first chapter of 1 Samuel.

She wept and prayed because of her barrenness. Her husband loved her, but could not alleviate the anguish she experienced. And her husband's other wife tormented her.

Hannah promised that if God would give her a son, she would give him to God for all of his life. God heard her cry, understood how she was suffering, and answered Hannah's prayer by giving her a fine baby boy.

She never forgot that her son, Samuel, was an answer

to prayer. She even gave him a name that would remind her that he was God's gift to her. "Samuel" sounds like the Hebrew phrase meaning, "I asked the Lord for him." Each time she spoke his name she recalled how God heard and answered her prayers. Hannah remembered her promise, too. She loved and cherished her son, but she knew he was not hers to keep. Samuel was to belong to God.

A struggle must have raged in Hannah's heart because she would soon have to take her dear Samuel to the temple and leave him with Eli, the high priest. As she nursed Samuel, she probably felt the bitter sweetness as she kissed his forehead and held him to her breast. Samuel often lay sleeping beside her, warm and close, but the day of separation kept approaching. Every day brought closer the time for the fulfillment of her vow. The struggle may have grown more intense if Hannah knew about Eli's immoral sons, who "were wicked men" and "had no regard for the Lord" (1 Samuel 2:12). Hannah would be sending her son into a corrupt environment. Dare she turn her son over to Eli's care? How could she entrust her beloved Samuel to Eli, whose own sons were growing up to be so wicked? Hannah had vowed to give Samuel to God; she knew she must keep her vow. Perhaps she thought about not being close enough to comfort Samuel when he fell ill, or to talk with him at night before he went to sleep. She would not share each day Samuel's excited chatter about his lessons, nor his disappointment when his day went poorly. She would not be near to warn Samuel about Eli's wicked sons or to explain God's plan for him.

As she pondered, she may have realized that prayer was her only recourse. She could have an impact on Samuel's life through prayer, and experience the power and goodness of God as He answered her prayers.

Since we can pray anywhere and at any time, our

prayers are our most effective means of influencing our children. Only prayer knows no boundaries. Neither separation, nor the present spiritual condition of the child, nor a mother's lack of experience in prayer can hinder the lasting effects of prayer.

The Bible does not record any of Hannah's prayers for Samuel after she left him at the temple, but certainly a God-fearing woman who prayed so earnestly for his birth would continue to pray faithfully for his protection and growth to maturity.

After Hannah left Samuel with Eli, she sang the song of praise to God recorded in 1 Samuel 2:1-10. This song confirms our understanding of Hannah as a woman of spiritual depth. She knew how to praise, as well as how to ask. Only women who have spent time alone in God's presence—agonizing, asking, and searching, and receiving comfort as well—pray like this. Jesus said, "Ask, and you will be given what you ask for. Seek, and you will find. Knock, and the door will be opened" (Matthew 7:7, TLB).

Last year, a young Japanese man who stayed in our home gave me a lovely *himetemari*—a ball of thread made by Buddhist mothers as they pray for their daughters. Japanese mothers wind the finest, most brightly colored silk threads around the ball, making an intricate design as they pray earnestly for their daughters' future happiness and prosperity. These balls are passed on from generation to generation. The new robe that Hannah stitched each year for Samuel (1 Samuel 2:19) may have corresponded to this. Each new robe could have represented Hannah's petitions rising lovingly before God as she wove and stitched. When she completed a robe, perhaps she eagerly anticipated taking it to Samuel and seeing in his growing life the answers to her prayers.

What about us? Are the gifts we prepare for our children stitched and formed in prayer?

Samuel "grew up in the presence of the Lord" and "continued to grow in stature and in favor with the Lord and with men" (1 Samuel 2:21,26). This reminds us of Jesus' boyhood: "Jesus grew in wisdom and stature, and in favor with God and men" (Luke 2:52). Isn't this what we want for our children too? Prayer can enlist God's help on their behalf.

Is your child keeping bad company? Are you concerned about various unpredictable influences in his life? What character qualities could you ask God to develop in your child's life? Is he responsive to God's Word? Is he conscious of God's presence? Is he seeking to obey God? Is he trusting God in prayer?

In each of these areas you can be an instrument for bringing about change in your child's life. Like Hannah, you can have a significant influence through prayer.

A Promoter of the Kingdom

God has entrusted the advancement of His kingdom to men and women whom He calls shepherds, laborers, harvesters, ambassadors, teachers, stewards, servants, and soldiers. To do this work, God looks for those who care about His concerns, His honor, and the advancement of His kingdom. This is the attitude we want our children to have, and we should pray to this end.

In the 1800s, Annie Rossell Fraser shared her concern for those without Christ with her children, and she prayed that at least one of them would become a missionary. Her third son, James O. Fraser, went to China and pioneered a work among a totally unreached people in the rugged mountains of China's interior.

Although it wasn't easy, Annie Fraser gladly gave her son to God's work. In *Behind the Ranges,* the account of James O. Fraser's missionary life, we read,

To part with such a son was a heartache that only such mothers can understand. Yet it was a willing sacrifice. "Jim, Dear, I am the happiest woman in London today," she wrote in the little note he carried with him. And it was a joy that continued, because the loneliness was for Jesus' sake. "I could not pour the ointment on his blessed feet, as Mary did," she said. "But I gave him my boy."[5]

Annie Fraser kept praying for the cause of missions. She organized prayer groups to support her son's work in China, and labored faithfully in prayer and correspondence to promote God's kingdom.

We, too, should pray for laborers. "The harvest is plentiful, but the workers are few. Ask the Lord of the harvest, therefore, to send out workers into his harvest field" (Luke 10:2).

When I pray that our children will serve Christ and further His work on earth, I don't know what form their service will take. God may choose to have them promote His kingdom as missionaries in the jungle, from a pulpit with a stained-glass backdrop, from an invalid's bed, or as teachers, farmers, secretaries, or plumbers. The job description is immaterial. It is their heart for the kingdom that counts.

Your children can become a part of this much-needed labor force, if you will pray. Ask God to use your children to further His kingdom. No spiritual cause can be advanced apart from prayer. In *Quiet Talks on Prayer,* S. D. Gordon reminds us, "You can do more than pray, after you have prayed. But you cannot do more than pray *until* you have prayed."[6]

Just as Jesus asked the mother of James and John, so He now asks us, "What is it you want?" What's your answer?

"Until now you have not asked for anything in my

name. Ask and you will receive, and your joy will be complete" (John 16:24).

How often do you find yourself quickly uttering a simple, "Lord bless Charlie" kind of prayer? Too often our prayers are dull and uncertain instead of vital and dynamic. So let's consider a few more practical ideas to help us accomplish something for God through prayer.

USE THE BIBLE AS YOUR PRAYER BOOK

The prayers of Moses, David, Hannah, and many others can be our patterns as we learn more about how to pray. In the New Testament, the prayers of Paul for his spiritual children are especially useful in learning what to ask for our children. Copy Paul's prayers on index cards and use them as your models as you pray for your children. Consider passages such as these: Ephesians 1:17-19 and 3:16-19; Philippians 1:9-11; Colossians 1:9-12; Philemon 4–7; and 2 Thessalonians 1:11-12.

Allow the lives of Bible characters to guide your prayers. You might ask for protection from Satan's deceitful tactics so they will not yield to temptation as Adam and Eve did, for example. You could also pray for the right mates for your children, just as God gave Eve to Adam.

Let your quiet time reading provide stimulation for your prayer times. When you read God's Word, look for qualities that honor God and ask Him to build these qualities in your children's lives. First Corinthians 13 is a good place to begin: patient, kind, not envious, not boastful, not proud, not rude, not self-seeking, not easily angered, forgiving, truth-loving, protecting, trusting, hopeful, persevering.

Write down specific requests that come to mind as you read. This will help you pray purposefully, and keep your mind from wandering. Also write down the Scripture reference that inspired your request, and leave space to record how God answers. Recording and reviewing answers will strengthen your faith.

Pray with a partner. Perhaps your husband—or another mother from your neighborhood, church, or Bible study group—would join you in praying for your children. Special power is unleashed when believers unite to pray.

"Again, I tell you that if two of you on earth agree about anything you ask for, it will be done for you by my Father in heaven. For where two or three come together in my name, there am I with them." (Matthew 18:19-20)

E. Stanley Jones, a missionary to India for fifty years, explains how his mother and another woman prayed regularly for him.

When my mother was dying, she called Miss Nellie and said to her: "These years I have prayed for Stanley. Now I am going. I'm turning him over to you, for you to take up my vigil of prayer for him." Miss Nellie said to me years later: "I've been true to the entrustment." I cannot think of Miss Nellie without thinking of that phrase: "I've been true."[7]

We, too, can be true to the entrustment as we faithfully pray for our children. We may affect their salvation, their spiritual growth, their character development, and their service for the cause of Christ—all through prayer. E. M. Bounds' words remind us how much is at risk:

Woe to the generation of sons who find their censers empty of the rich incense of prayer; whose

113

fathers have been too busy or too unbelieving to pray, and perils inexpressible and consequences untold are their unhappy heritage. Fortunate are they whose fathers and mothers have left them a wealthy patrimony of prayer.[8]

QUESTIONS FOR REFLECTION OR DISCUSSION

1. What would you like God to do for your child?
2. Read Forbes Robinson's prayer again. List four important requests he made.
3. What does it mean to pray "for the salvation of your child"?
4. What is one specific idea about prayer that you can apply to your life this week?

NOTES
1. S. D. Gordon, *Quiet Talks on Prayer* (New York: Grosset & Dunlap, 1904), p. 12.
2. As quoted by Joseph W. Cochran, in *Heroes of the Campus* (Philadelphia: Wesminster Press, 1917), pp. 88-89.
3. Albert C. Outler, ed. and trans., *Augustine: Confessions and Enchiridion*, vol. 7 (Philadelphia: Westminster Press, n.d.), p. 74.
4. Dr. and Mrs. Howard Taylor, *Hudson Taylor's Spiritual Secret* (Chicago, Ill.: Moody Press; China Inland Mission edition, 1958), p. 13.
5. Mrs. Howard Taylor, *Behind the Ranges* (Greenwood, SC: Lutterworth Press, 1959), p. 25.
6. Gordon, *Quiet Talks on Prayer,* p. 16.
7. E. Stanley Jones, *A Song of Ascents* (Nashville: Abingdon Press, 1968), p. 44.
8. E. M. Bounds, *Purpose in Prayer* (Chicago: Moody Press), pp. 7-8.

Chapter Eight

"DO YOU LOVE ME, MA?"

I wanted to laugh and cry at the same time. Lynn Johnston's comic strip, *For Better or Worse*, hit me where it tickled and hurt simultaneously.

Picture a harried, frustrated mother hunched over the sewing machine, pins in mouth, and a string of expletives filling her speech balloon.

In the next frame, her son stands innocently at her side and asks, "Do you love me, Ma?"

At that moment the sewing machine is malfunctioning and Mother's frustration level is rising.

"Mama, do you *love* me?"

Mother grunts. A blank expression is on her face as she fiddles with the errant machine.

Her son tries again, tapping his mother's leg, hoping to get her attention this time. "Ma? Ma? Ma? . . . do you *like* me then, Ma?"

Suddenly she turns on the boy with wild eyes and exclaims, "Yes! I'd *like* you to get lost!"

Her startled child reels back and races off, dissolving into tears. Mother slumps dejectedly and reflects, "Something tells me I could have handled that better."

Ever had that feeling? I have—and so has my friend Susan.

LOVE—WHEN THINGS GO WRONG

Susan's daughter, Lana, wanted a new dress for her birthday. Together they chose the pattern, the fabric, the buttons, and lace and ribbon for trim. Susan was happy to make the dress even though her schedule was full.

She couldn't start on the dress until nine that evening. By then she was very tired, and several telephone calls interrupted her progress. She cut out two left sleeves, then, after the dress was cut out, remembered that she had forgotten to preshrink the fabric. The bobbin thread often bunched up and broke as she sewed. Everything was going wrong.

Then Lana appeared in the doorway. "Mommie, I had a bad dream. I'm scared!"

Jumping up angrily, Susan screamed, "I don't care, get into bed and don't come out here again!" Lana shuffled back to bed, sniffling and feeling hurt and unloved.

Susan was confused by how she had reacted. Resentment and shame grew within her. She loved her daughter, but her actions didn't show it.

Like Susan, I have planned some "fun deal," and then ruined it with impatience and grumbling. I was like "The Mother with Good Intentions."

A certain woman loved her family, so she planned an elaborate and extravagant picnic with silver serving dishes, fine china, her best crystal, and a fragrant floral centerpiece. The picnic menu included steak au poivre flambé à la crème,

116

spinach soufflé, and baked Alaska. With everything perfectly prepared, she led her family through ankle-deep mud to the picnic site, and spread the blanket on an ant hill.

Since it is impossible to savor baked Alaska with ants swarming up your leg, I suspect her planning and hard work didn't achieve what she hoped. All of us, parents and children alike, find it difficult to rise above certain circumstances—and an unloving attitude can be every bit as obtrusive to a picnic as an army of ants.

As I've thought about the role of love in my mothering, I've been stimulated by 1 Corinthians 13, which I have paraphrased:

If I keep my house immaculately clean, and am envied by all for my interior decorating, but do not show love in my family—I'm just another housewife.

If I'm always producing lovely things—sewing, art; if I always look attractive, and speak intelligently, but am not loving to my family—I am nothing.

If I'm busy in community affairs, teach Sunday school, and drive in the carpool, but fail to give adequate love to my family—I gain nothing.

Love changes diapers, cleans up messes, and ties shoes—over and over again.

Love is kind, though tired and frazzled.

Love doesn't envy another wife—one whose children are "spaced" better, or in school so she has time to pursue her own interests.

Love doesn't try to impress others with my abilities or knowledge as a mother.

117

Love doesn't scream at the kids.

Love doesn't feel cheated because I didn't get to do what I wanted to do today—sew, read, soak in a hot tub.

Love doesn't lose my temper easily.

Love doesn't assume that my children are being naughty just because their noise level is irritating.

Love doesn't rejoice when other people's children misbehave and make mine look good. Love is genuinely happy when others are honored by their children.

You may also find it stimulating to review this chapter, meditate on it, and rewrite it in your own words.

But what is love? National Public Radio aired a program called "Better Loving Through Chemistry." According to this program some scientists now believe the "in-love" feeling is a chemical reaction inside our bodies triggered by certain stimuli. But the Christian concept of love is best illustrated by the Supreme Example of love. No love in history begins to compare with His love—love that made God become man, leaving the unsurpassable splendor of heaven to come to earth as a baby born in a stable. What love! How can we comprehend or explain it? We can't! Shouldn't this convince even the most hardhearted of us that God loves us? He limited Himself for our sakes. The God of the universe came to serve as man—He healed, He preached, He comforted. And He was not only a servant; He was also a sacrifice. He willingly died on the cross in my place, and in your place. Jesus did not focus His mind and efforts on Himself. Instead, He emptied Himself of all privileges and rights. Christian mothers must pattern their lives after His example—the supreme example of the loving servant.

MOTHER'S RIGHTS?

Our society does not easily identify with Jesus' example of giving up His rights. Instead we assert our rights: "women's rights," "children's rights," "gay rights," "minority rights." New categories are constantly being added to the list.

Mothers, too, can grasp for their rights, but sometimes they find their capacity to love is dissipated by their firm resolve to protect those rights. A mother in one cartoon is seen tacking up a sign: "Mother goes off duty at 8 P.M." That seems fair enough, doesn't it? After all, who has longer hours than a mother? Should we perhaps organize or unionize to ensure our right to some time off?

The world urges us, "Assert yourself," "Fulfill yourself," "Liberate yourself," "Please yourself," "Satisfy yourself." But Jesus says, "Die to yourself." It seems like a step backward. Our lives are to be sacrificed for others, not in some sort of melodramatic martyr complex, but in following the daily challenge of Christ's example. Listen to Jesus' words:

> "I tell you the truth, unless a kernel of wheat falls to the ground and dies, it remains only a single seed. But if it dies, it produces many seeds. The man who loves his life will lose it, while the man who hates his life in this world will keep it for eternal life." (John 12:24-25)

Christ commands us to love even as He loves. "My command is this: Love each other as I have loved you.

119

Greater love has no one than this, that he lay down his life for his friends" (John 15:12-13). Love is laying down our lives for others. Just as our Lord Jesus Christ gave His life for us, so we are to give our lives away for others. To love is to die. When most of us think of dying for someone, a dramatic picture usually comes to mind. Perhaps you envision yourself leaping in front of a friend to take the bullet intended for him, or diving into the path of a speeding truck and pushing a child clear. Certainly these are examples of love, but Jesus calls us to a way of dying that is less romantic. Each day we have numerous opportunities to live for others and not ourselves. We may serve others and die to self by being dedicated to seeking the good of others.

Paul instructed us, "Be imitators of God, therefore, as dearly loved children and live a life of love, just as Christ loved us and gave himself up for us as a fragrant offering and sacrifice to God" (Ephesians 5:1-2). I have learned a lot about Christlike love by observing my husband. Roger's unselfishness is a constant challenge to me. Most people return home from a hard day's work feeling they deserve some peace and quiet—time for themselves before entering into family life—time to unwind with the newspaper or by watching the evening news. But Roger has a wonderful ability to change gears as soon as he comes through the front door. He makes us his recreation. He unwinds with us.

We appreciate how fully he enters into our day. He throws back his head and laughs with Graham about a cartoon. He bends to roughhouse with Beth's dog as Beth heads out the door with her. He listens attentively to Matt's plans for a treehouse. Nothing earthshaking, but we know we are loved.

I've asked him how he does it, and Roger says he just

loves being with us. Perhaps the ability to truly enjoy one another comes in proportion to the unselfishness of our love.

BATTLING SELFISHNESS

To be selfish means being "concerned chiefly or only with oneself, without regard for the well-being of others." Selfishness attacks all of us. We may face shortages of natural resources, jobs, and food; but we never lack selfishness. And no one needs to learn selfishness, because it comes naturally.

On a winter night the air in our bedroom is frigid.

I slide under the blankets, even covering my head, hoping my warm breath will thaw my nose. At last a toasty warmth envelopes me and I drift toward sleep.

Then a hacking cough disturbs the silence. I wait. Maybe it will go away in a minute or so. I struggle with ambivalent feelings: *Poor Beth, I guess I should fetch her some cough medicine. But I dread that shivering walk to the kitchen, now that I'm finally warm.*

If she coughs three more times I'll get up. Oh, Lord, please help her stop coughing. One more cough. "Please, Beth, stop coughing," I whisper. Two more coughs. That makes three. I can delay no longer. Reluctantly I pull on socks and a robe and drag myself to her aid.

I've acted in this scene, with slight variations, many times. Sometimes a child's need interrupts my bath, reading a good book, a sewing project, or an interesting phone call. The interruption may be in the form of tears, a bloody nose, an argument, a piercing scream, or an explosion in a back bedroom. Whatever form it takes, I resent it.

How often I've resented these violations of my

"rights," when I should have thanked God that I could be there when my children had a need. Recently I found a diary page I wrote during a time of discouragement some years ago. My complaint was entitled, "What Bothers Me About Being a Mother."

1. The demands on my time.
2. Serving them over and over.
3. Never finishing my work.
4. I'm frustrated by not knowing how to handle problems. (Should I spank or comfort, make them play alone or do something with them?)
5. No time for my interests.

Throughout the years, when my children were still at home, these five complaints continued to pinpoint most of the struggles I faced. Perhaps you can identify with me. But have you noticed that four out of five of these complaints are "me-centered"? Only number four is truly concerned with doing what is right for them.

But learning how to love others as Christ has loved us means putting the needs of others above our own. Here are some ways we can do this.

DEMONSTRATING MOTHER-LOVE

Tell your children you love them. Everyone likes to be told they are loved. Whisper it in their ear. Write it on notes popped in their lunch box, or pin notes to their pillow. Tell them casually as they leave for school. Or draw them aside and say, "You are *very* special to me; I love you very much."

Use terms of endearment. Call your children by pet names: sweetie, honey, love, buddy. Affectionate words change the spirit and tone of the exchange for both you and your child.

Show affection. Babies need to be touched as well as fed to survive. As your children grow they continue to need tenderness. Hugging and kissing come to mind immediately, but older children (particularly boys) may be embarrassed by this. Find ways of expressing love without making your children feel self-conscious (especially if you have not shown much affection in the past). Wrestle with them on the floor, touch their shoulders as you pass their chair, or squeeze their arm and say "Love you" as they leave for school.

My boys let me kiss them if I pretend I'm the Kissing Monster. I chase them around the house, wrestle them to the floor, and plant one on them. They even chase me to kiss me if I pretend disdain because their faces are dirty.

Navigator staff member George Sanchez has said, *"Hold a crown a couple of inches above their heads and encourage them to grow into it."* This could be accomplished in many ways, such as writing them a letter telling them what you appreciate about them. List a combination of physical, mental, social, and spiritual qualities. Include areas where they show effort even if they remain unsuccessful—something like, "Thanks for trying to get the wrinkles out of the blankets when you made your bed." Don't take your children for granted.

You might write a note like this, for example:

Dear Jane,

 I love you, and I want you to know some things I really appreciate about you.

 You are very pretty, but I think you are even prettier inside! I've noticed how generous you are

123

with your things and your money, and I know God loves generous people, because He is generous too.

Your hard work on your multiplication makes me proud, especially since I know math isn't your favorite subject. That makes me admire your effort even more.

Also, I want to thank you again for hostessing Mrs. Smith until I got home the other day. You were so thoughtful to fix her a glass of orange juice and to sit with her and talk.

Daddy and I are more and more convinced how special you really are.

Love, Mom

If your children are too young to read for themselves, read the letter to them.

Respect your child's worth as an individual. You might find the following checklist to be helpful. Do I listen to my child? Do I consider his feelings and ideas? Do I give him sufficient recognition, and numerous compliments? Do I accept him for himself? Do I avoid comparing him with others? Do I handle discipline privately (not in front of his siblings or friends) and fairly? Do I allow him an appropriate amount of privacy?

Play with your child. Remember to play your child's way and not your own—even though you may find it frustrating to play hide-and-seek with a child who jumps out from behind the couch and yells, "Here I am!" the moment you finish counting. Remember your ultimate goal: Play helps you build a relationship with your child. Don't underestimate the value of ten minutes of driving toy cars in the sand or of coloring pages with your child.

Listen. Put down your dish towel, and bend down to your child's level. Look him in the eye. With your facial expressions and voice, enter into his enthusiasm, disappointments, or discouragements. Your tone of voice is especially important.

Be available when they want to talk. We fool ourselves if we think we can relegate conversation totally to time slots that are convenient for us. A wise mother figures out when each child likes to talk and makes herself available at those times. Does he bubble over right after coming home from school? Is it the quietness of bedtime that seems to loosen his tongue? Or maybe he likes to sit on a stool in the kitchen while you cook dinner.

Plan for them. "What would you think of this idea? This summer I'd like to spend lots of time with you. Since the city pools are free, we could swim every day. And would you also like to try some new arts and crafts projects?" My children's response to this question was *very* positive. Including them in the planning helped make the plan work. "In order to do this I'm going to need some help. I will still have just as much work to do. If we all work together we can get all our chores done in the morning. It won't take long if everybody helps. Then we can go to the pool, and when we get back we can do arts and crafts, or play." The plan worked and we had a great summer.

Share with your children your plans for spending time with them. Get their ideas and reactions. This helps them feel more loved and secure.

Forgive them. As parents, our practical demonstration of forgiveness—or the lack of it—will largely shape our children's ideas about forgiveness, including God's forgiveness. This makes it extremely important that I not only experience God's forgiveness personally, but that I also learn how to mirror a forgiving spirit in my interaction with the children.

125

When God forgives, He "blots out" our transgressions and forgets our sins (Isaiah 43:25). We too must say, "I forgive you," execute the proper discipline, and then deal with that child as if his misbehavior never happened. Even if we can't erase the problem from our mind, we can refuse to allow it to affect our relationship with the child. But if we continue to remind him of the time he left the rake out overnight and it rusted, we have not forgiven him completely.

I was talking on the phone one day when I heard a dull thud in the living room. I cut my phone conversation short: "Marilyn, I'll call you back. I think our living room is being bombed." Seconds later two of the children stood before me sheepishly. Nearby was a shattered pot, damp potting soil spread over the carpet, and a mangled plant with exposed roots. I was counting to ten slowly. "Mom, I knocked it over," one of them said. "I'm really, really sorry. Will you forgive me?" I will always remember the relief I felt when I first experienced God's forgiveness. God wiped my slate clean and gave me a new beginning. Now one of my children stood before me asking me to give him a fresh start. Paul's words came to mind: "Be kind and compassionate to one another, forgiving each other, just as in Christ God forgave you" (Ephesians 4:32). Another verse came to mind: "For if you forgive men when they sin against you, your heavenly Father will also forgive you. But if you do not forgive men their sins, your Father will not forgive your sins" (Matthew 6:14-15).

My course was clear. I must forgive. I had no alternative. I said, "I forgive you." Then I sent him running for a towel and the vacuum cleaner. I helped him repot the plant, scoop up as much dirt as possible, and left him to run the vacuum.

As a Christian I must learn to be especially good at forgiving. My own forgiveness is tied to my willingness to forgive others. I can't afford to be unforgiving. And just as it is important to teach our children to ask for forgiveness, so parents also must sometimes ask for their children's forgiveness. Even mothers aren't perfect. Often, I must remember to say, "I'm sorry, Beth, I wasn't listening. Will you forgive me please?" Or, "I handled that poorly, Graham. I shouldn't have yelled. Will you forgive me?"

A final suggestion is to *keep current on the worries and joys of each family member.* Here are some ideas for doing this.

Show interest by asking questions like, "How are things going at school, Charlie?" or "What are you thinking about these days?"

Be understanding. Say, "I understand. Math was hard for me too." Or, "I can see how you would feel that way."

Allow them an opinion—even if it is different from yours. Share your failures, fears, and joys with them: "I think I hurt Mrs. Tully's feelings. I said the wrong thing. I'll call her back and apologize." Or, "I feel fearful about giving this talk tomorrow. I'm nervous about speaking to so many people. Will you pray with me?" Or, "This is great. I'm finally seeing progress on my sewing project."

Allow your children to realize you are a person too. Like them, you are vulnerable. This makes you approachable—one to whom they can come without reproach because you, too, have fears, dreams, and discouragements.

A word of caution: Remember that this sharing is for your child's benefit, to make it easier for him to express his feelings. But it could be unwise to communicate some concerns to your child, such as difficulties in your relationship with your husband, money problems, or fear about losing your job. These should be shared with another adult.

Also, don't pounce on them with your ideas and solutions. Use restraint. Listen to them, and don't try to solve all their problems for them.

Show love and acceptance by your tone of voice and facial expression.

Be available when they want to talk.

Be courteous. Love is not rude. Remember to say "please" and "thank you" as you talk with them.

Comfort them. Pull them close when they have a bad day. Kiss their tears, rub their backs when they feel tense, hold them on your lap.

Encourage them. Make a list of "Ten Things I Like About You"—such as, You notice things I miss, You have a nice laugh, You make people feel welcome at our house.

Make time. "Could I spend some time talking with you tonight, Mom?" "Sure," I replied. But that "sure" didn't come easily. It never does. Making time for our children costs something, but it is an expression of our love for them.

I'm not suggesting that mothers shouldn't have time for themselves. They should. Nor am I saying that a mother's work has no end, or that mothers shouldn't be served as well as serve. But our life's focus can either be "me" and "my rights," or seeking the good of others. And the Lord commands us to love.

Mary, my friend, is a runner. When she began running about five years ago she had difficulty running even a city block. Now she regularly runs five miles a day and competes in races, after working diligently to build up her endurance and speed.

This year Mary and her two teenage daughters decided to run together in a local 7.8-mile race. Her youngest daughter Karen had never even run that far before. Mary and her girls ran together almost daily to train for the race.

On the day of the race, I thought of Mary, and pictured her straining for the finish line, trying for her best time ever.

Later that afternoon I called her. Mary, instead of running on her own, had stayed back to run with Karen and encourage her. Karen finished the race, and Mary's excitement focused on Karen's success. Karen ran farther than she ever had before.

Mary put Karen's success above her own. Seeking another's welfare means giving our lives away on their behalf like this, running with them to encourage them rather than running ahead and expecting them to keep up with us.

Questions for Reflection or Discussion

1. What do we learn about God's love through the life of Jesus Christ?
2. How would you describe the kind of love God wants us to show to our children?
3. What are three ways you could show love in your family this week?
4. What personal characteristic (selfishness, anger, self-pity, impatience, etc.) most often keeps you from showing love to others?

Chapter Nine

A TEACHER AT HOME

Gordon Parks was the youngest of fifteen children born to a poor farmer in Kansas. He never completed high school, yet he has written several books and directed films. He never took a music lesson, but has composed a symphony and several sonatas.

Gordon Parks attributes his broad-ranging accomplishments to his mother, Sara Parks—a poor, uneducated black woman who often had a Bible tucked under her arm. Just before her death when Gordon was fifteen, she called him to her and said,

> Son, I think you're going to be a great man. But I want you to work at it. Mind your sisters. They'll tell you what is right because I've taught them what is right. Then go north. Take advantage of everything. Do things a little better than the best. Do things a little bigger than the biggest. But always remember this place—I want this house to be your learning tree.[1]

Have you ever thought of your home as a *learning tree*—a place where you provide spiritual and intellectual stimulation for your children? Do you consider your home as a setting in which to encourage their dreams and inspire their creativity? Is your home a safe place for sounding out new ideas? Is it a launching pad from which your children can go out to explore the world beyond?

In *Roots of Success,* authors Leslie Elliott and Trudy Schlacter explore the role of the mother in the lives of gifted children. Almost without exception the mothers of these boys and girls involved themselves intensely in their children's lives to encourage, stimulate, and develop them. This earnest attention by the mothers was evident regardless of their social or economic backgrounds, and seemed to be a common denominator among these gifted individuals.

In *Behind the Ranges* we gain insights into the home life of pioneer missionary J. O. Fraser. His mother taught her children drawing and music, and passed on to them her own concern for missions. Annie Fraser studied the Scriptures diligently in order to effectively communicate spiritual truth to her children. The Fraser family even published a monthly magazine, and together pursued interests such as photography and cycling.

While still a boy, J. O. Fraser caught from his mother a love for missions, for learning, and for life.

Can we dismiss Sara Parks and Annie Fraser as exceptional women, too gifted to be models for us? Are their ideas only for the few mothers who possess extraordinary talents or vision? No! They are examples for all of us.

THE PARENT AS TEACHER

A man was trudging through the snow toward the corner bar for his nightly round of drinks. Suddenly he became aware of soft steps crunching the snow behind him. He turned and saw his young son leaping from footprint to footprint, placing his small boots in each print made by his father's strides.

Perplexed, the father asked, "Son, what are you doing?"

"Following in your footsteps, Dad."

Appalled, the father lifted his son to his shoulders and headed home.

Parents are teachers. Our children will learn from us good or bad, positive or negative. We are their teachers whether or not we accept this responsibility.

Deuteronomy 6:5-7 is a key passage to study to determine what God wants us to teach as well as how He wants us to teach our children.

> Love the Lord your God with all your heart and with all your soul and with all your strength. These commandments that I give you today are to be upon your hearts. Impress them on your children. Talk about them when you sit at home and when you walk along the road, when you lie down and when you get up.

When I realize God calls me to actively teach my children, I view my teaching responsibility more seriously and keep alert for anything that will help me in my teaching—for learning opportunities. Instead of the dry taste of duty, I find a sense of encouragement, excitement, and challenge.

God outlines the qualifications for the parent-teacher, suggests the curriculum, and tells us how, when, and where to teach. Any mother can improve her ministry to her family by applying these ideas.

QUALIFICATIONS FOR THE PARENT-TEACHER

God doesn't require a teaching certificate for parents, or even a diploma. He demands no previous experience, special gifts, or talents. But He does have His own school and training program. In God's school, the parent-teacher must first become a "student," "follower," and an "obeyer." God *does not* require perfection, but only a deliberate, conscious, step-by-step obedience to what He shows and teaches His students. The parent-teacher is not required to reach a certain level of competence in obedience before he begins to teach his children, but rather he must keep developing in obedience as he or she teaches. Learning and teaching are lifetime pursuits. No mother ever reaches a point where she may stop learning and devote herself totally to teaching. Learning and teaching go hand in hand.

THE PARENT-TEACHER'S CURRICULUM

I was lying on the beach watching our three children wading in knee-deep water when the relaxed tranquility was interrupted by a loud, grating threat. "If you don't shut up I'll stuff a sock in your mouth!" I sat up and glanced over my shoulder at an irritated mother scowling at her six-year-old daughter. "Does it work?" I asked lightly. Slightly embarrassed, she laughed and said, "I don't know. My mother always said it, and I guess I say it now without thinking."

Have you ever caught yourself sounding like your mother? I have. When I think of some of the sayings that get passed unthinkingly from generation to generation, I wonder if we should not be more selective.

Some of the sayings from the past might well be allowed a quiet death. Others are more worthy of being handed down.

Whenever I hear a mother say, "I'll be so glad when school starts," I remember my mother saying, "I hate to see school begin. The summer went by so fast. I'll miss having you around." My mother's comment always made me feel loved. I knew she enjoyed having me around. I want to pass that same kind of feeling on to my children.

What do we want to communicate to the next generations? What concepts do we want to see deeply ingrained in our children and their children? How would we like our sons and daughters to complete the sentence, "My mother always said . . ."?

Thankfully, God has already indicated the most important things we should pass on, and why. God commissions parents to tell their children who He is and what He says about life. Why? So our children may enjoy an abundant and long life (Deuteronomy 6:2-3).

God says much about how we are to relate to one another, so we teach, train, and discipline our children to treat others with kindness, generosity, grace, forgiveness, and a spirit of reconciliation. God asks only that we treat others as He has treated us. No more, no less. The Bible speaks amply of God's kindness, generosity, grace, and forgiveness. He wants us to forgive others because He forgives us. He wants us to be generous with others because He is generous to us. Good interpersonal skills help our children now and with friends, classmates, coworkers, and spouses in the future.

Ongoing bickering and fighting among family members is not inevitable. We can use times of quarreling and tears as opportunities to teach our children to resolve conflict. Our job is to teach our children about God and His ways, and to train them in the spirit of reconciliation because we are part of a kingdom based on forgiveness.

When one of our children came to me angry or in tears complaining of some mistreatment by a sibling, I followed a set of steps outlined in Scripture to teach and train toward obedience and reconciliation.

1. Help the offended child to articulate what happened and express how it made him feel. "Ronnie hurt my feelings when he said I look like a goat" or "It made me angry when Jeri got into my stuff."
2. Help them get their emotions under control. Coach them to use a soft voice (Proverbs 15:1) when they tell the offender how the offense made them feel (Matthew 18:15). Remind them that the goal is reconciliation.
3. Talk with the offender before the offended child comes to confront the situation. Do whatever teaching or coaching is necessary to help them see their offense, the need to say, "I'm sorry. Please forgive me" (Matthew 6:14-15) and seek reconciliation. Often they feel offended in some way as well and need steps 1 and 2.
4. Have the children talk with each other for the purpose of reconciliation. Monitor the situation. For example, if the offended child shared his hurt and the offending child said, "Tough!" then, more teaching or discipling is needed.

At first, the process is very demanding on the mother, but in time they resolve their conflicts with little coaching.

Our broad curriculum, therefore, includes teaching first of all *who God is,* and second, *what He teaches about life.*

Clear? Yes. Simple? No. The depth and breadth of God's character are inexhaustible. The ongoing revelation of His work as Creator and Sustainer has no end. My teaching task is so large I sometimes feel I've been assigned to carry the Atlantic Ocean across land to the Pacific Ocean a teaspoonful at a time. Where do I start with such a big job?

CLEAR AIMS

Writing out a few simple aims helps me grasp my task more clearly. Written aims help me to set a direction and to provide a basis for planning, implementing, and evaluating.

When I use the word *aim,* I do not want to infer that we can determine our children's destiny. We cannot. Neither are these aims the only basis by which we decide if our parenting has been successful or not. Our children have minds of their own. They will ultimately take their own direction in life.

But establishing aims can help us to maintain perspective and a consistent direction in our parenting. Without clear-cut, specific aims, I too easily lose sight of my goal.

The benefit of well-defined aims for the Christian family is obvious, but where do we start in making and accomplishing those aims?

The first step in developing aims for your children is to *determine what goals God has already set for His people.* As we read the Bible we can be alert for the aims God has in mind, and we can make these the basis for our specific aims for our children.

God's aim for us is Christlikeness. Christ is the standard for maturity. As we consider our aims for our children, we must evaluate those aims against God's goal for them—Christlikeness.

J. H. Jowett wrote in *Things That Are Needful,* "You must come to your child with a vision of the man you would like him to be." What is your vision for your child? Does it match God's thinking?

I use several questions to compare my values regarding my children's growth and maturity with God's value system:

- ◆ Do I value godly character above financial success, physical beauty, or scholastic and athletic achievements?
- ◆ What do I compliment and correct my children for? Do my remarks lead them to think that good grades are more important than acquiring them honestly? Do I comment more on my child's grooming than on his character? Do I compliment kind deeds, thoughtfulness, obedience, and gentleness as much as pretty faces, good grades, and touchdowns?
- ◆ Is performance more important to me than attitude? Can I appreciate a smeary mirror that my child tried to clean because he sincerely wants to be helpful? Can I manage to remain gracious if my child spills the tray while serving me breakfast in bed?
- ◆ Are the same things important to me that are important to God? Our values are important because they shape our aims. If they don't agree

with God's thinking, they may do more harm
than good.

Discuss your values and goals for your children with
your husband. Consider spiritual, mental, physical, and
social goals for them. Compare your vision and values
with God's goal—Christlikeness.

Reading books and talking to other parents about
the subject can also be helpful. Take advantage of other
people's ideas.

Finally, write out your own general and specific aims
for each of your children.

IDEAS FOR AIMS

The book of Proverbs qualifies as a parent's handbook
and can help you determine good aims for your children. It begins with a father's urgent instruction to his
son (1:8), and concludes with a mother's teachings
(31:1). Scattered throughout the book is the phrase *Listen, my son,* constantly reminding us of the scope of this
parental instruction. Topics covered include how to
choose friends, what company to avoid, diligence, self-
control, and careful speech—qualities and abilities that
are crucial for developing true maturity in your
children.

Above all, the aim of Proverbs is to promote wisdom,
for "wisdom is supreme" (4:7). Mothers may want to
study Proverbs to help them *define* wisdom, to note wisdom's *characteristics* and *benefits,* to compare wisdom with
the contrasting characteristic of foolishness, and to
determine the steps we must take to become wise. Reading Proverbs can help stimulate your thinking about
what you would like to see in your child's life.

As we determine the goals that will guide our

teaching, we can benefit from examining other parents' goals for their children, such as this list that one mother compiled:

- ◆ Trust and believe in God.
- ◆ Love God and walk humbly with Him.
- ◆ Love and serve people.
- ◆ Love the Bible—God's word.
- ◆ Pray and believe God for answers.

Another mother focused on more detailed behavioral patterns:

- ◆ Submission of their wills
- ◆ Control of their tongues
- ◆ Acceptance of discipline
- ◆ Physical independence
- ◆ Ability to deal with pain and failure
- ◆ Ability to relate to others effectively
- ◆ Ability to choose companions wisely
- ◆ Ability to wait patiently
- ◆ Ability to work hard and well
- ◆ Ability to show respect for Dad
- ◆ Ability to show respect for others

You and your husband may find it helpful to discuss your long-range parenting plans, and even to write out specific goals in areas such as these for each of your children:

1. A personal relationship with God.
2. Godly character: obedience, generosity, purity, holiness, joy, friendliness, integrity, faith, faithfulness, patience, love, kindness, servanthood.
3. Healthy personality: inner happiness based on

self-assurance and trust in God; self-respect and respect for others; a sense of self-worth; the ability to act responsibly; a sense of purpose; and the ability to laugh at himself.

4. The ability to live effectively with others in his group: openness; showing loyalty, understanding, and forgiveness; and assuming responsibility for the well-being of others.

5. The ability to think critically, especially in setting and maintaining good standards and values.

6. The ability to work creatively and to express himself as a unique individual.

7. Common sense and good judgment.

As a family you may want to identify a few basic qualities you would like to characterize your family. These are five our family has worked on:

1. Providing an atmosphere of love and an awareness of God's presence. Making our home a haven of rest and security. Cultivating a growing consciousness of Christ's headship in our family.

2. Building strong family ties. Viewing home as the place we would rather be. Building healthy relationships and always showing respect for one another even when disagreeing.

3. Making our home a learning center. Working together to help each individual fulfill his or her potential. Giving each other the freedom to fail and to make mistakes.

4. Building the family team by involving everyone in planning and achieving family goals. Taking pride in one another—supporting each other, showing mutual trust and faithfulness.

5. Being a center of witness to the world. Maintaining an open testimony to friends and strangers by word as well as by life.

If the ultimate aim of our teaching is Christlikeness, then conversion must be a primary aim in our work with our children. They cannot grow in Christlikeness unless they personally decide to follow Christ.

All our input, no matter how well we teach, will be as superficial as make-up unless our children come to Christ personally. Our best teaching and training will never accomplish the deep work in their lives that only comes through spiritual rebirth.

While conversion is essential, remember also these observations:

1. Young children want to please. If they sense a pressure to accept Christ, they may go through the motions out of their love for us. But this is not true conversion. We want to provide the information and the nurturing without any coercion.
2. They must never feel that our love or acceptance hinges on their response to Christ.
3. We must acknowledge our powerlessness to make anything spiritual happen in our children's lives. Our best efforts won't make our children Christians. Only God can do that.

How and Where to Teach

The Hebrew word for *teach* or *impress* used in Deuteronomy 6:7 may be translated several ways, including to point, to pierce, to prick, to teach diligently, to whet.

These words suggest something more than a dry presentation of the appropriate material. Our teaching should be full of life and force, full-bodied and savory enough to whet our children's appetites for God. God can help us do this as we try to impart truth to our children.

We can teach our children as we sit around the table at meals, huddle together by an open fire, relax with them over a good book, accompany them to school, hike a wilderness trail, or stroll leisurely through a shopping center. God wants us to be alert to opportunities to teach as we tuck our children into bed, sponge them with cool water when they are ill, or lie on our backs on the lawn entranced by dancing leaves overhead.

This teaching must be natural and often spontaneous. God doesn't call us to give a polished presentation. He wants us to teach in the midst of the common, everyday situations we all face as we share life with our children.

Our son Graham once built a tall tower with his blocks. Higher and higher he went, until his edifice swayed, tottered, and came crashing down. The clatter of blocks was followed by a torrent of angry tears. Graham was overcome with frustration.

I remembered Proverbs 25:28—"Like a city whose walls are broken down is a man who lacks self-control."

So I sat among the blocks and talked with Graham. After using the blocks to build a circular wall, I asked, "Graham, do you know why they used to build a wall around a city?"

We spent several minutes discussing the importance of a strong wall for a city's protection in olden times. Then I repeated Proverbs 25:28 and suggested that his anger when his blocks fell made him like a city with its walls broken down—an easy place for the enemy to enter. Together we prayed that God would help him with his self-control.

At another time, after a four-year missionary assignment, we found ourselves back in the United States with a considerable list of needs. We had only a sewing machine and a rocking chair of our own. We needed a house to live in and furniture and appliances to outfit it.

We made our needs the family's prayer list. At meals and bedtimes and while traveling in the car, we specifically prayed about the items on our list. As God provided for our needs, we began scratching items off the list. We watched our list shrink as God graciously and often spectacularly supplied a house, a refrigerator, furniture, and more.

In our first month in our new home, two of our children prayed and asked Christ into their lives. I believe the tangible evidence of God's provision and tender care—so obviously experienced in those days—had made God very real and desirable to them.

Another teaching opportunity came one Sunday on our way to church. A guest was riding with us. Out of the blue one of the children in the back leaned forward and asked, "Mom, what is a prostitute?"

After a simple explanation, we talked about Rahab, the prostitute in Jericho whose story is told in Joshua 2:1-21 and 6:22-25. We reviewed how she feared and obeyed God after learning about Him. God then honored her by including her name in the lineage of Christ (Matthew 1:5). I also reminded the children that Jesus was kind to prostitutes, and forgave them if they would leave their sin behind and trust in Him. Afterward our guest whispered, "I'm glad they asked you and not me."

Often the opportunities to teach come masked as

interruptions. Roger and I lay reading in bed one night when Matt complained he couldn't sleep. Although it interrupted our reading time, we invited him to join us. Letting him share my propped-up pillows, I handed him *The Living Bible,* quickly filled him in on what was happening in King Ahab's life, and then continued reading in another Bible. A little later we sent Matt off to bed and turned out the lights. Next morning, Matt had some interesting insights into the passage, and said he had read more about Ahab. The time he spent reading with us had whetted his appetite for more.

One three-day weekend the children were looking forward to a day off from school. But on Saturday night the flu struck. All of us were affected. Matt and Beth joined us in our bed to watch a football game on television. At bedtime we moved Beth to her own bed, but decided to leave Matt in our bed. Matt and I would sleep in our room, Roger in Matt's.

In spite of the sickness, Matt and I had some excellent conversations that long night. Together we gave thanks for being sick under the best possible circumstances. We had a comfortable bed, clean sheets, ice to suck, and ginger ale to sip. And we were reasonably sure the sickness would pass in another day or so. We chatted about the Southeast Asian boat people, and the poor of India—most of whom have no bed, clean water, or even blankets. Remembering others who were in worse circumstances helped us to be grateful in our sickness.

At two A.M. that night, Matt still couldn't sleep. "I'll be so glad when morning comes," he said. "I know I'll feel better when it is light."

His comment reminded me of Psalm 130:6—"My soul waits for the Lord more than watchmen wait for the morning." We could empathize that night with a man standing a lonely watch, longing for the first glimpse of the sun. Did we wait for the Lord's return with the same longing? We discussed this thought briefly between moans and groans.

Later I asked Matt, "What do you know about Job?" We talked with each other about this man who knew terrible sickness and trouble, and yet remained faithful to God. Thoughts of Job challenged us in our relatively mild affliction.

All this was nothing profound, but it ministered to both of us that long night. The Scriptures gave us a God-ward look when our eyes would have focused naturally on ourselves.

Developing As a Teacher

For most of us the ability to recognize and use everyday happenings to teach our children doesn't come naturally. It is a skill that must be developed and honed. Like most skills it requires conscious, diligent effort if we are to realize our potential as teachers. I have begun thinking of myself as a teacher. This has made me more alert to ideas that would be helpful in communicating God and bringing spiritual truths alive for young minds, as I seek ways to adapt my teaching to my child's age level and interests.

Have you noticed how Jesus, the Master Teacher, often used familiar objects in His teaching? He used lamps, vines, and mustard seeds to teach spiritual truth. In His wisdom He knew we learn best when we begin with what is known and familiar.

When teaching our preschoolers about God, I found it helpful to follow Christ's method. Matt and Beth were around three and two when I began asking God for ideas that would enable me to enlarge their understanding of who He is. To teach them about Jesus as the good Shepherd, I pretended to be the shepherd, and the children were my sheep. I gave each child a new name (a sheep name). They crawled around on the floor and "ate grass." I led them to a pool of cool water (a rug) for a drink, put bandages (rags) on their legs, showed them affection (kissed them and scratched their heads), searched for them when they were lost (behind the couch), and chased away imaginary bears, wolves, and lions. The children enjoyed this activity and I saw their understanding of a shepherd's ministry to his sheep enlarge and deepen.

They also liked to hear the simple adventure stories I told in which the shepherd would discover one sheep missing, and then find it and gently carry it home. Sometimes I told the stories as if I were the shepherd, and at other times from the lamb's point of view: "I am a lamb. My name is Rono. I live with my mother and many other sheep. A good, kind shepherd takes care of us. One day. . . ." The story varied in details, but the lost lamb was always rescued by the shepherd from some misfortune.

Role playing, arts and crafts, music, field trips, reading, Scripture memory, storytelling—all these teaching tools can be used to help children move from the known to the unknown in learning spiritual truth. And don't forget everyday situations as well.

I once stood in the rear of an Okinawan shop waiting to pay for my purchases, when three-year-old Matt asked if he could wait for me outside. I said yes, but when I stepped out onto the sidewalk he wasn't there. A feeling of panic overtook me. Which direction should I look? Was he kidnapped? What should I do? Where could he be?

I didn't know enough Japanese to ask if anyone had seen him, or to describe him to the Japanese shopkeepers. I prayed. One lady and I exchanged sign language for "little child—lost" (at least that's what I was trying to say). She sent me back in the opposite direction. Not sure whether she understood or not, I hurried along, praying as I walked.

Up ahead I saw a lady carrying Matt. He had told her that we had a yellow station wagon, and she was helping him find it.

As we talked about it later, Matt said he was a lost sheep and he knew the good Shepherd would find him. For a long time afterward Matt often talked about Jesus helping me find him when he was lost. The teaching about our good Shepherd had taken on a new depth of meaning for both of us.

I used variations of these teachings on the good Shepherd over a period of six to eight months. It wasn't an everyday thing, of course, but a thread running through my time together with the children.

Try developing an idea using this same teaching approach yourself. Consider teaching about Jesus as the bread of life, or as the light of the world. Think of as many ways as possible to communicate this truth: Bible verses, art, music, drama, literature, and storytelling. Consider ways to involve them personally and to use all five of their senses: hearing, smelling, seeing, feeling, and tasting. Above all, relate Jesus simply and interestingly to their everyday experiences.

When I picture a mother wisely using all of life to impress God's truth on the lives of her children, I am profoundly challenged. I want to do all I can to make my home a "learning tree."

Such effective, timely teaching must be an overflow

of our lives. We can't share with our children what we don't know ourselves. The right words won't automatically roll from our lips. Our readiness depends on our intake of the Bible and our fellowship with God.

God's command to teach our children is an assignment with enough breadth and depth to occupy the talents of the most able woman. It requires full use of her abilities, energy, and resources. But she will find opportunities to teach in every nook and cranny of life— opportunities far more numerous than we might think. So, let's roll up our sleeves and plunge in. We have so much to learn, so much to teach. May God bless our feeble efforts and accomplish His purposes in our children's lives.

QUESTIONS FOR REFLECTION OR DISCUSSION

1. What example or idea from this chapter motivates you to teach your children?
2. List five things you would like to pass on to your children and grandchildren.
3. Describe an opportunity to teach that you missed this week. What might you do about it next time?
4. What familiar objects in your home have you used to teach a lesson to your children? What are some others you could use?

NOTE
  1. As quoted by Marian Christy, in "His Mother Planted the Seeds of Gordon Parks' Success," *The Seattle Times,* 20 February 1980, p. B-9.

Chapter Ten

TEACHING THROUGH DISCIPLINE

"Who spanks mothers and fathers?" one of our children asked after receiving a spanking.

"God is our Father, and He spanks us," I replied. I tried to explain that discipline is a part of life for parents as well as children, but it wasn't until a few weeks later that God provided a vivid illustration that satisfactorily answered the question for them.

One of our family rules was never to go into a neighbor's yard without first asking the neighbor's permission. One afternoon during a family ball game, the ball sailed over a concrete wall into another yard. Contrary to family policy, Roger vaulted over the five-foot wall. Unexpectedly, the neighbor's dog, Gypsy, raced toward him with uncharacteristic vengeance. As Roger grabbed the ball and leaped over the wall to escape Gypsy's attack, his shin struck the sharp edge of the wall and he tumbled into the alley. When he sat up, blood was flowing from a painful gash on his leg.

Roger hobbled to the house and we worked, unsuccessfully, to stop the bleeding. Finally, we headed for the hospital emergency room.

Later that evening Roger was stretched out on the couch at home with his leg elevated on a stack of pillows. He called the children to him. "You asked how God spanks mothers and fathers," he said. "This is how. I made a rule, but I didn't obey it. I was like the witch in a book by C. S. Lewis, *The Magician's Nephew,* who thought she was above the law. God had to discipline me."

WHAT IS DISCIPLINE?

Discipline is not a pleasant word. But when we understand God's purpose and plan for discipline, we won't be resentful when it comes to us, and we can more effectively use it in training our children.

Discipline extends far beyond prevention and punishment. In speaking of God's discipline in Deuteronomy 11:2, Moses cites "his majesty, his mighty hand, his outstretched arm." Have you ever thought of these in relation to God's discipline? "You were shown these things," Moses said, "so that you might know that the Lord is God; besides him there is no other. From heaven he made you hear his voice to discipline you" (Deuteronomy 4:35-36). See how broad discipline can be?

God's discipline does not emanate from cruelty or revenge, but from love. I came to understand the close link between love and discipline the year I taught fourth grade. When I interviewed for the job, the principal said, "This is the worst class in the school." I took the job, and the class members lived up to their billing.

As I stood before that group of children I could see their potential being drained away by their destructive behavior. *Poor Jerry, shy and quiet—how will he ever find*

*what he needs in this class? And Ralph—he's his own worst
enemy. His life is a wild, downhill ride toward ruin. And Mike
. . . and Marco . . . and Debbie . . . and . . .*

How I longed to make a difference, to turn life
around for those fourth-graders, to excite them about
learning, to awaken them to their potential, to give them
a dream. I had wonderful ideas (I thought) to make
learning exciting and to inspire them to achieve. But
their rebellious behavior prevented me from implementing most of my plans. Sometimes I would weep
because they seemed determined to destroy their
chances for growth.

Before I could begin to teach and build and inspire,
I had to control and police. They could not learn until
they first submitted to my authority.

When God looks at us and sees the potential of our
lives, the richness of our possibilities—does He ache
inside because we are unable to receive His marvelous
plans? Sometimes God must use pain and hardship—
from illness to clogged plumbing and flat tires—to get
our attention, because He wants to awaken us to our
possibilities. Because He loves, He disciplines. In fact,
His discipline proves that He loves us (see Hebrews
12:6-11).

In the same way, disciplining our children must
reach beyond correcting undesirable behavior and punishing offenses. Discipline is positive. Discipline is training. Discipline helps our children become what God
created them to be.

Teaching and discipline are inseparable. Unless
accompanied by instruction, the various methods of discipline used by parents become, at best, shortsighted,
and at worst, harsh or dangerous.

Guidelines for Discipline

As a mother you undoubtedly know how children often need loving discipline at precisely those moments when we feel least like doing it carefully and correctly. Our nerves are on edge. Our minds are confused, our emotions churn, and anger rises within. At times like these we need most to pray, think clearly, and use restraint as we discipline.

Use the following suggestions to help you pinpoint sources of frustration at moments like these. I've also found it helpful to write out my feelings in order to deal with them more objectively.

Recognize the internal struggle. Children inherently want to please, but they also have a sin nature. Like us, they fail, make mistakes, and do wrong. Imperfection runs in the family. To err is human. Don't expect flawlessness.

Identify the issue. If I'm feeling irritated and victimized by my child, I need to identify *what* is bothering me and *why.* I ask myself, "What does he do that bothers me? Why does he do it? Why does it bother me? Is he really doing something wrong or is he merely acting his age? Does it bother me because it inconveniences *me,* or makes more work for *me?* Am I tempted to discipline my child, not for his good or to help him grow, but for *my* pleasure, *my* convenience, and *my* best interest?

Pausing to think like this will usually help you define the real cause of your irritability. Be thorough and specific and honest. Perhaps talking over your feelings later with a friend or a more experienced mother will help restore your sanity.

You might even consider writing out a checklist to consult at difficult moments such as when your child

won't stop crying. Your family's pediatrician can also rec-
ommend a reliable guide to childcare to use as a ready
reference.

Have realistic expectations. It is unfair to expect a two-
year-old to act like a six-year-old, or to want an eleven-
year-old to take on adult responsibilities. Nor can I justly
demand silence from my children when I have a
headache.

If you feel uncertain about what you can fairly expect
from children at particular ages, you may find help in
Arnold Gesell's *Infant and Child in the Culture of Today*
(Harper and Row). This book is a classic volume on early
childhood development. Dr. Gesell profiles each age
group, outlining their general capabilities. Naturally, no
child matches the profile perfectly, but the book can
make you more observant and alert to your child's stage
of development.

Be consistent. Most parents agree that consistency is
important in teaching and training children. But what
do we mean by consistency?

Does it mean always dealing the same way with the
same offense? I don't think so. Recall how God has
helped you in some specific area of your life, such as
honesty or patience. I suspect, if your life is like mine,
that at times God used the Scriptures to instruct, or con-
vict, or encourage you in this area. At other times He
used people to confront your shortcoming. At another
point He used the Holy Spirit within you to whisper,
"You need my help if you are going to change. Now con-
fess your sin and let Me control you." And still again He
used someone to encourage your progress: "I have seen
tremendous growth in your life this year."

God does not always teach us with a slap on the wrist
or a straightforward rebuke. He is more creative than

that. But God is consistent. He faithfully and diligently works beneath the surface of our lives to conform us to the likeness of Christ.

Years ago, I told one of the children that I would spank him anytime he committed a particular infraction. This child received a couple of spankings for this disobedience, and one day came to me crying, "I did it again. I didn't want to do it, but I did it."

As we headed for the bedroom for the spanking, the Lord reminded me how often I wanted to do right, but sinned again. I remembered how I fail again and again in areas where God is at work in my life, and I felt a deep empathy with this child.

Once inside the bedroom I said, "I understand how you feel. I often feel that way too. You don't need a spanking. You want to do right. You just need God's help. So let's pray." We knelt together and asked God to change us and help us do what is right and good. It was a time of earnest prayer for both of us. And I believe I was consistent in dealing with the child's wrongdoing.

Sometimes consistency in discipline means a spanking, sometimes a talk, sometimes praying for or with our children. The methods will not always be the same, but they will be consistent if they all have the goal of moving a child toward Christlikeness.

Likewise, consistency in discipline does not mean never changing your mind or reversing a decision. What a bitter trap we parents fall into when we feel we must hold to every dictum that passes our lips, regardless of its soundness.

Suppose my child asks, "Mom, may I play at Julie's house today?" I am busy and distracted, and find it easier to say no than yes. Cautiously, my child says, "Mom, was there a reason? We were going to finish the decorations for the class party."

I think, *Was there a reason for saying no?* Not really. But I decide "consistency" and my "honor" are at stake. "The answer is no," I tell my daughter, "because I said no."

Our decisions need not bear the stamp of permanence. We are human. We make mistakes and poor decisions, and we should not be bound to them.

Talk to your children. Develop the habit of talking with your children even when they are babies. When our children were babies, my husband walked them around the house naming things for them: "Lamp . . . window . . . plant . . . chair." Outside he named flowers, leaves, animals, and rocks. I even heard him explain how a tape recorder works to our one-year-old son.

Inform your children of the schedule, since giving them an idea of what to expect seems to make them more ready to comply as it prepares them mentally for what lies ahead: "Tina, when I finish sweeping the kitchen, we will read a story, and then take a bath." This preview teaches Tina sequence and patience, and gives her time to adjust to the idea of a bath.

Give an older child opportunities to make decisions. Ask, "Tommy, do you want your bath before or after the story?"

Many children grow up hearing few words directed to them except commands and put-downs. What a shame to always hear, "Sammy, shut up," "Sammy, hurry up," "You spilled your milk again," but never to hear, "What a good job you did, Sammy," and "I think you are terrific." Children learn through praise and encouragement as much as from correction and command.

What have you said to your child today? Were they positive words? Kind words? Commendation is a part of discipline, so keep alert for specific reasons to thank and praise your children.

Provide opportunities for your child to achieve success. A

157

sense of accomplishment provides energy and motivation. Think of tasks your child can do with reasonable success. Acknowledge his efforts and rejoice in his victories. Make sure he doesn't think you notice him only when he does something wrong or can't do something at all.

Follow through. It is not enough to tell a child what to do; we must follow through to ensure obedience.

When I ask my child to pick up his toys, I am providing an opportunity for him to learn obedience or disobedience. My request requires that I make sure he has put away his toys. If I find he has not done as I asked, I must act to make certain he completes the task. I may stoop down and make eye contact, and say, "Honey, I asked you to pick up these toys. Please finish the job before you do something else." Or set the kitchen timer for two minutes and make a contest out of the work. Different approaches work for various personalities and ages.

In the doctor's waiting room one day I heard a mother call to her little daughter, "Jessica, come here," "Jessica, Mommie said come here," "Jessica, come here right now!" But the mother never left her chair to enforce her command.

Jessica turned a deaf ear to her mother because she knew her mother well. Experience taught her that the commands were nothing more than words. Nothing would come of them. Jessica had concluded she could do as she pleased.

My son beside me gave me a glance and whispered, "Her mother should make her obey." He was right. But this mother found the *Ladies Home Journal* on her lap more compelling than her commitment to her daughter.

This mother had failed her child. She wasn't unkind to her, but she wasn't loving her either. "He who spares the rod hates his son, but he who loves him is careful to discipline him" (Proverbs 13:24).

Provide diversions. In this situation in the waiting room, I think Jessica's mother should have gone another step beyond getting up and leading her daughter back to her chair. Since she did not want Jessica wandering around the waiting room, getting into other people's purses or crumpling magazines, the mother should have provided a diversion to occupy her daughter. She could have held Jessica on her lap and looked at pictures in the magazine. Or she could have brought along toys or books from home, or played patty-cake with her. It is unrealistic to expect a two-year-old to sit placidly at our feet while we relax with a magazine.

Diversion can be a helpful tool. Suppose three-year-old Johnny heads toward his sister's sewing basket. Instead of saying, "No, Johnny, don't touch," you could divert Johnny's attention to something else. You could say, "Johnny, let's go find Daddy," or "I'll read you a story now." Or you could grab him and roll on the floor with him, tickling and wrestling him. How much easier and more pleasant this is than having a head-on collision of the wills.

Of course, battles of the will cannot be totally avoided, but they can be carefully chosen. What a shame to get caught in a head-to-head confrontation over an inconsequential issue.

Suppose your efforts to divert Johnny from his sister's sewing basket make him even more determined to have it. He takes a deliberate stance and pulls away from you to get to the forbidden basket. You have reached a point of no return. You and Johnny face each other in a battle of the wills that YOU must win. Johnny must submit his will to yours. You must follow through. His willful disobedience cannot be overlooked.

The issue in Johnny's case is not the sewing basket; the issue is disobedience, disrespect, and defiance, and we cannot sidestep it.

SPANKING

In an age when child abuse is the major killer of children under three years of age, many conscientious parents may hesitate to spank their children at all. But I believe spanking has a place in the nurturing of our children. "Folly is bound up in the heart of a child, but the rod of discipline will drive it far from him" (Proverbs 22:15).

Since the value of spanking is dissipated if it becomes the routine method of discipline, spanking should be used sparingly. And it should be done with restraint and control. Never spank in anger. Control the force and limit the swats and place them carefully on the fleshy area of their bottoms.

Do not put off a spanking until Daddy comes home. Take care of incidents as they happen—for "when the sentence for a crime is not quickly carried out, the hearts of the people are filled with schemes to do wrong" (Ecclesiastes 8:11).

A spanking should be administered in private and be accompanied by teaching and explanation. Afterward, the child should be assured of your love for him and your concern for his best interests.

REWARDS

The idea of training by rewards has been popularly espoused as a primary method for disciplining children. In behavior modification, desirable behavior is rewarded and undesirable behavior is ignored or punished. A few jelly beans may be promised as a reward when a child completes a task such as making the bed or finishing his homework.

Being a nation of pragmatists, we believe if anything "works" it must be right. But training children primarily on the basis of rewards has intrinsic dangers. My child may grow up to be easily led by whoever is handing out the rewards. He might make decisions based on personal profit instead of a sense of right and wrong. Or he may come to expect reward as a confirmation and natural result of right action, when, in fact, he may be required at times to suffer for doing good (see 1 Peter 4:12-13).

As you can see, unless we teach our children what is right, what is good, and what God expects, they will be unprepared to make moral choices and to develop deep personal convictions.

Rewards can be a legitimate motivation. God promises rewards to the faithful. Just last week I gave Graham the last piece of fudge for putting away the garbage cans without being asked. But rewards are not always immediate. In fact, sometimes the right behavior by followers of Christ is met first by beatings, imprisonment, and even death, with the rewards coming later.

I'M IN CHARGE

God gives me the responsibility for teaching and training my children, and the authority needed to do the job. He commands my children to honor and obey me. I am in charge. I have the responsibility, plus God's backing.

Many mothers are worn ragged by hassles which occur over and over, sapping their energies and causing them to feel trapped and exasperated. Many of these hassles began as a small attitude or an overlooked

161

disobedience, and have gradually become like a giant snowball chasing the retreating mother downhill. Stop, take a firm stance, and say to yourself, "I'm in charge."

Recently, I found myself with pent-up frustration as I faced such a snowball. I was asking the children to pick up their messes, but getting no results. *I'm talking, but nobody's listening.* Then the thought registered: *I'm in charge here.* I began to consciously follow through on every request by checking to ensure the children were obeying.

Another mother, Linda, asked her eleven-year-old daughter, Sarah, to begin her homework right away because the family would be visiting friends for the evening. Sarah said, "But, Mom, I told Janice I'd go over to her house." Linda sighed. Sarah interpreted Linda's sigh as acquiescence, and rushed out the door.

Linda then turned to Ryan, her six-year-old. "Ryan, I'll run your bath water now. You take your bath while I finish getting ready." After drawing Ryan's bath, Linda headed for the kitchen to iron her dress. She remembered Sarah's homework, and phoned her to come home. Sarah begged to stay another thirty minutes, and Linda faltered: "I really think you should come home now. You know you have homework. Oh, all right—but I still think you should come home."

As Linda began pressing her dress, Ryan sauntered through the kitchen still unbathed. Linda's temperature rose. "Young man, if you don't get into that bathtub by the time I count to ten. . . ."

Linda finished her ironing and headed for the bedroom to dress. As she passed the bathroom, she noticed Ryan kneeling in his underwear beside the tub playing with his bathtub toys. She glanced at her watch. She yelled, "Ryan, get in that tub this instant," and rushed into the bedroom to slip into her dress. She knew her husband would be home soon. Where was Sarah?

Linda phoned Sarah again and said, "Get home on the double, young lady, before I. . . ." The story goes on, but I'll stop here.

Linda forgot two important things. First, she is in charge. She not only *may* make decisions, but she *must* make decisions. If the schedule will not allow Sarah to play at a friend's house today, Linda must make the decision and enforce it. It may be an unpopular decision, but part of Linda's responsibility as a mother requires that she take charge. Although Linda is a capable woman, her reluctance to take charge in her family makes her appear weak, indecisive, and easily manipulated. Her children find her easy prey. When Linda dropped her "I'm in charge" banner, her children snatched it up for themselves before it hit the ground. Linda's frustration grew.

Second, her failure to follow through with Ryan to make him do as she asked cost her time and drained her emotionally. The few minutes spent getting Ryan into the tub would be well worth the time and effort.

Take heart, mothers. The care you give your child, the responsibility you take for his training, and the love you express through diligent discipline are not in vain. You are a partner with God in the nurturing of your child.

No one said it is easy, but it is worth it. "Discipline your son, and he will give you peace; he will bring delight to your soul" (Proverbs 29:17).

QUESTIONS FOR REFLECTION OR DISCUSSION

1. What impresses you most about the way God disciplines His children?
2. Describe your most frustrating discipline problem. What are the elements that make it confusing or difficult?

3. Consider the statement: "In the same way, disciplining our children must reach beyond correcting undesirable behavior and punishing offenses. Discipline is positive. Discipline is training. Discipline is helping our children to become what God has in mind for them." List several adjustments you need to make in your thinking, attitudes, and actions.

4. How does the realization that God has given you the responsibility for training your children affect the way you look at the job?

Chapter Eleven

ROOTS AND WINGS

Under a delightful watercolor painting I read this caption: "The best thing parents can do for their children is give them roots and wings." I like that idea because I want to give our children more than survival skills—I want to give them soaring skills as well. Both "roots" and "wings" are important if our children are to develop to their full potential.

When I think of *roots*, I mean providing a foundation of security and stability for my children. Just as the nourishment and stability of a plant depends on its root system, so human life is sustained and stabilized by its roots.

The greatest source of nourishment I can give my children is, of course, a relationship with God Himself. As they grow "down" into God and allow the tentacles of their being to become firmly entwined with Him, they will have the best possible roots.

My relationships with God, my husband, and my children create an environment that can either help or hinder the development of this good root system for my

165

children. A secure, loving home is the fertile ground their tender roots need.

While the depth of my children's lives is dependent on their roots, the height to which they can soar is dependent on their *wings*. The idea of wings connotes *creativity, appreciation, laughter,* and *freedom*.

Wings come as my children reach up to God and allow Him to set them free from the fear of others, free from self-imposed limitations, and free to become all God intended when He created them. Wings lift my children above the routine and the mundane. From this altitude they gain a fresh outlook on life, seeing above their circumstances and being sensitive to the delights of life God has given.

Our children allow us to share their wings when they call us to the window to see a spectacular sunset, or share an unusual twist of plot from the book they are reading, or go one step farther when setting the dinner table by lighting it up with candles.

When I think of giving my children wings, I think of doing "extras" beyond meeting their basic needs. I want to enrich and surprise them, stimulate and refresh them, delight and enchant them. I want them to see our home full of life because God is there.

WHY GO TO ALL THE TROUBLE?

God created all of us to have these wings. Look around you. Why did God make giraffes with long legs and even longer necks? Why did He bother to put those funny little knobs on the tops of their horns? Why didn't He color them solid beige instead of painting them in a masonry pattern? Why are there golden lions, profusely colored butterflies, spotted leopards, and shimmering peacocks?

Why such diversity and beauty? Because God created us to soar with wings of imagination and appreciation. He "richly provides us with everything for our enjoyment" (1 Timothy 6:17).

As mothers, we can tap our own creativity to enhance the development of our children's wings—so they can enjoy all that God provides.

"But I'm not very creative," you may say. You may surprise yourself. First of all, you are made in the image of God, the Creator of all. You have a creative capacity, though it may not be well developed.

Second, your commitment to your children will release the kind of creativity you need to stimulate the development of wings. If you have read *Swiss Family Robinson* or *The Little House on the Prairie,* you know how creative people can be when their survival is at stake. The families in these books coupled their personal creativity with the few resources they had to work with, and they did much more than merely survive.

Third, creativity can't be used up. Your creative "muscles" may be weak from disuse, but they can be strengthened with a little effort.

When I was an art student I became aware that the more art I created, the more ideas I had. But since my marriage I have done very little painting—and when my husband suggests I spend a relaxed few hours at it, I stare at a blank canvas. I cannot think what to paint. To get my creative juices flowing again, I could benefit from visiting an art gallery or taking a painting class.

The same is true for mothers—we can improve our creativity in mothering if we are given creative ideas and models. Perhaps some of the ideas that have worked in our family will stimulate your creativity and encourage the growth of your children's wings.

SURPRISES

Surprises can add zest to life, demonstrate our love, and delight our families. Variety is the spice of life, so use variety to bring an element of surprise into your family.

When I was a girl, my mother would often rearrange my room at spring and fall housecleaning time. Since my bedroom was small, the options were limited, but even small changes didn't go unnoticed. I always loved sleeping the first night in a rearranged room.

The next time you pull out the bed to vacuum behind it, rearrange the furniture. If that isn't possible, try one of the following ideas.

1. Put away the bedspread and make the bed with clean sheets and a colorful blanket. Turn the sheet back (my children call this a "company fold") and pin a note on it.
2. Move a plant into their room or make a small flower arrangement for their dresser.
3. Decorate the room for an approaching holiday. At other times of the year you can cut butterfly shapes from construction paper, let the children decorate them with markers, crayons, or paints, and then hang them on strings from the ceiling.
4. Clip a few pictures from a magazine and tape them to your child's door.

Here are other ideas for surprises:

Rotate toys. I noticed that whenever I sorted through our old toys and put them in a box for the Salvation Army, the kids would suddenly become enchanted with a toy they hadn't played with for months. They would often persuade me not to dispose of the beloved relic.

One day it occurred to me that perhaps absence does make the heart grow fonder. I divided the children's toys into three boxes. I stashed two of the boxes in the top of the closet and left one available for play. Every two or three months I would rotate the boxes. A new box of toys always received a warm welcome.

When we moved from Arizona to Washington, I started a "rainy day box" for those rainy winter days in Seattle. As I packed for our move, I gift-wrapped old puzzles, games, coloring books, children's magazines, and a few stuffed animals and put them in a decorated box.

Later when I heard the complaint, "I don't have anything to do," I would get down the "rainy-day box," allow the children to choose and open a package, and play with the forgotten toy.

Each of our children has one "junk drawer" in their dresser or chest. It is the place for anything small they want to save. Occasionally (when the drawer is too full to close) I ask the children to sort through their "junk" and toss or trade unwanted items, and reorganize what they intend to keep. This cleaning project often turns up "treasures" that recapture their interest (shells from a vacation at the beach, an old letter from a friend, a school paper with a good grade).

Kidnap your children. One day Roger nonchalantly called the children into a bedroom one by one, grabbed them and blindfolded them, and had them sit quietly on the bed. Then we led them to the car and drove them, still blindfolded, to a surprise. Your children will enjoy the excitement of such a ride and also the surprise at the end—maybe a merry-go-round ride at the park, a pond with ducks to feed, or an ice cream store.

Go on a treasure hunt. First, write clues on small pieces of paper. They may be simple or difficult, depending on the ages of your children. They may rhyme or be in riddle form. Each clue in turn leads to the next clue and finally to the prize! Among other things, I have had our children hunt for each course of a meal, or for a note promising something after dinner.

SPECIAL ACTIVITIES

The number of special activities you can involve your children in is endless. I'll suggest a few of our family favorites. (Remember that activities for small children should not be considered merely as ways to occupy them while you sew or clean. Some special activities require adult participation and supervision.)

When our children were small, we kept a child-size table and two chairs in the kitchen. The children often used their table for snacks and crafts. Once I tore up an old sheet to make the right sized cloth for their table, then made potato stamps by cutting a potato in half and carving a simple design in the end. The children dipped the carved end into a small dish of India ink or thick poster paint, and then stamped the design on the tablecloth. This project kept them busy for some time.

SCHOOL AT HOME

Every morning after I finished the breakfast dishes, we would have "school" in the kitchen. Family photos show Beth at age one and Matt at two finger painting in the kitchen schoolroom. I learned to tape their paper to their high chair trays to keep it from moving around while they colored or painted. Finger-painting paper can be submerged in water and then smoothed on their trays.

170

Three framed finger paintings done by our children when each was under three still hang in our home. I like them, and so do our guests. Several parents have marveled at their bright colors and fresh designs, since many children that age will rub any combination of colors together into a brownish purple mix. My children were no exception. But when they painted, I waited until they had something attractive, lifted that sheet of paper away, and smoothed another wet sheet onto their tray. In this way they had something they could be proud of to show Dad, and they also learned to stop when they had created something pretty.

Some evenings, after the children were in bed, I would clip colored pictures from catalogs and magazines and put them in a box. During school I would let the children tape these pictures to sheets of paper to make collages. (It works well to make little circles out of the tape and stick them lightly to a plastic saucer. That makes it easy for the children to tape up their own pictures.)

We would make these pages into a book to show Daddy, or tape a page on the refrigerator or bedroom door. These pages were excellent for teaching new words, so we "read" these pages together and identified babies, trees, and dogs. Several days later I pulled the pictures off the paper and replaced them in the box to be reused another day. As the children grew we began painting with brushes, and cutting and gluing. We learned colors, shapes, and textures. We practiced the alphabet and learned numbers. As they got older I made up actual worksheets for them to write and draw on.

Boxes also make wonderful learning toys. Give your child a large cardboard box to play with and he can turn it into a train, sports car, house, or spaceship.

171

The disguise closet is another favorite. In the bottom of the linen closet I kept a box of miscellaneous clothes, shoes, jewelry, wigs—anything with possibilities. Our children and neighbor children have made frequent visits to the disguise closet over the years.

Even when our children were quite young, they wanted to help me in the kitchen. Sometimes it was difficult to think of a job they were capable of doing. Every job took longer, but my husband encouraged me to let them help, "Someday they will be a real help to you."

That day came when I was expecting between thirty and forty people for dinner and I was running behind. The menu was an Oriental dish that required washing and chopping several fresh vegetables. Beth, who was two, and Matthew, three, stood on chairs at the sink washing vegetables, and I chopped them up. Dinner was ready on time. It was the first of many times I said, "I couldn't have done it without your help."

Elaborate dinners can provide a fun way to include the children in planning and preparation. First choose a theme. The theme may be ethnic (a Japanese dinner eaten as you sit on the floor around your coffee table), historical (a celebration of Beethoven's birthday by listening to his music as you eat), or educational (a discussion of a current event). The children can make the centerpiece, hang streamers, make place cards, or come in costume.

Next, plan an appropriate menu. Some themes bring to mind certain foods. Other themes are unrelated to any particular food and can be a great way to make leftovers more interesting.

Write down the menu and display it to build anticipation. The menu can simply tell what you're having or it can develop the theme. For a pirate theme, for example, offer Seaweed Delight, Bilge Bread, Mermaid Munchies, and Pirate Parfait.

Decorate your table to fit the theme. For a cowboy dinner you might use the children's cowboy hat and a lasso as a centerpiece. Let them draw WANTED posters of each family member to hang near the table.

Carry out the theme with music: western songs for a cowboy meal or opera music for an Italian dinner. The library is a good source for ethnic background music.

One evening I announced that we were having a Tacky Dinner, and suggested that everyone change into something suitably tacky. Everyone, including our houseguest, rose to the occasion. We were a motley crew in clashing garments, inside-out shirts, and strange hairstyles. I set the table tacky too: mismatched placemats, flatware askew, and odd napkins. At each place a note folded by the napkin gave individual instructions: Keep passing the food, eat using only your knife, and talk to your food.

Consider using these two ideas for theme dinners to stimulate your thinking about other ideas:

European Peasant Dinner—the fruit as a centerpiece. Keep your apron on, and tie a scarf around your head. Serve hearty soup, cheese, bread, and fresh fruit. Pray together for Christians in Eastern Europe.

Buzzard Dinner—Serve hard-boiled "buzzard" eggs, toast, fruit cup, and spinach. Let the children dye the eggs. (I fill teacups halfway with water and use food coloring plus one tablespoon of vinegar for dye.) Cover a cookie sheet with foil and let them build a buzzard's nest with grass, twigs, old string, bottle caps—anything and everything. Arrange the dyed eggs in the nest and use that as a centerpiece.

Here are more ideas for creative touches at

173

mealtimes: Place a note under each person's plate with another family member's name on it. While the table is being cleared for dessert, each one can think of three things they like about that person.

Plan ahead to honor someone in the family on a certain day. Let that person choose the menu. The children might plan entertainment, such as a song, magic trick, or puppet show. Everyone could make personal greeting cards too.

Vacations

When our grown children get together I'm amazed how often vacation memories are the topic of the most lively discussion. My conclusion is that every family should plan and budget for vacations. Low finances shouldn't be the deciding factor. Be creative. Pray. Who knows what God might do for you.

Bedtime

Put the children in bed early one night and entertain them. Turn the light off in their room, but leave the hall light on and their bedroom door wide open. Each time you pass the door, do it in a different way: dance, swim, walk backwards, crawl, hop on one leg, or twirl.

For about seven years our children shared the same bedroom. Sometimes after we got them settled into bed, Roger and I would act out Bible stories and sing songs, or tell other stories. As the children grew older the stories became more complex. They especially liked serials. I would make up a story and stop at an exciting part— with the rest to be continued the next night. When we had a serial going, the children needed less persuasion

174

to get into bed because they couldn't wait to hear what would happen next. Some of these lasted more than a week.

One serial evolved as the result of a request for a love story. Our children were all in elementary school at the time. They had asked Roger and me to tell how we came to love each other. This evidently put them in the mood for a love story. As I made up the serial, I decided to use it to communicate principles which I feel are important in the areas of healthy relationships with the opposite sex, the selection of a mate, courtship, and marriage.

I started with John and Sylvia in high school and took them through a budding friendship, college, commitment to Christ, courtship, marriage, their first missionary assignment, and having children. Our children still mention John and Sylvia occasionally.

Plant pleasant thoughts in the minds of your children before they drift off to sleep. Quote Bible verses, talk about heaven, or describe a relaxing scene to think about—"Imagine you are lying in soft hay and a warm puppy is curled up beside you."

The success of many activities will depend on your child's age and interests. Our first two children loved books before they were one year old, while our last child was more interested in actively doing things than in sitting quietly to look at pictures and listen to words.

Try out different activities with your children at different times—if they seem uninterested now, try the same thing again in four or five months.

Building Resources

I pulled off my weeding gloves and looked at my watch. There was one hour until dinner, and I had forgotten to thaw the chicken. I rushed into the house, feeling irritated with myself for being so poorly organized. As I tried to think up an alternative menu, one of the children said, "Mom, I'm bored. Can you think of something to do?"

I straightened up from rummaging through the refrigerator and thought, *I need all my creative resources just to get dinner on the table.*

Then I remembered my "brainstorming list"—things to do with the children that I compiled on my last day alone with the Lord. Quickly I scanned the list. "Go get your hand puppets and rehearse a show," I said. "After dinner you can entertain the family."

My brainstorming list has helped us through troubled times more than once. I developed this resource by thinking up as many ideas as freely as possible. For example, I jotted down "Go to the circus" without any thought of whether our schedule was free or if we had enough money.

Think of as many fun things as possible that you could do as a family—or for the family. You might find it profitable to brainstorm with one or more people. The ideas of others often trigger new thoughts. Refer to this list not just at desperate moments, but whenever you want to give your family a lift. Here is a sample:

- ◆ Hike at Sabino Canyon.
- ◆ Picnic at the dunes.
- ◆ Have a surprise party.
- ◆ Send a care package to missionaries.
- ◆ Make Christmas ornaments.
- ◆ Visit a museum.
- ◆ Gather dried plants.
- ◆ Draw animals at the zoo.

◆ Serve a good meal.
◆ Write notes on napkins at dinner.
◆ Get in Mom and Dad's bed and read books.

Books

Books do much to develop our children's wings. We almost always are in the process of reading a book at our house. We read on the couch, in the car, or at the dentist's office—anywhere.

On summer evenings I sometimes spread a blanket on the grass in our backyard. The children, in their pajamas, lie on the blanket and listen as I read. Sometimes, in the enjoyment of that quiet, balmy evening, we read until the stars begin appearing.

If a trip to the library leaves you feeling overwhelmed by the vast numbers of books, ask the librarian for books that list some of the best children's literature. They give a short summary of the story and suggest the age group for which it would be appropriate. The librarian may have a listing of the Newberry and Caldecott award winners. These are books selected as the best-written and best-illustrated children's books of the year. If you find a good author, you can spend several months reading their works. Also, ask other mothers what their children have enjoyed.

Cheap Thrills

Have you noticed that few of these ideas cost any money? Some years ago we decided that we would concentrate on "cheap thrills" such as sunsets, walks, good books, and popcorn by the fire. A shortage of money need not rob you of meaningful—even delightful—family fun.

177

God created us to have wings—wings to rise above our circumstances, wings to find delight in simple pleasures, wings to enjoy what is beautiful, wings to lift another to new experiences.

QUESTIONS FOR REFLECTION OR DISCUSSION

1. What are you doing to give your children roots?
2. List five ideas mentioned in this chapter that you might use to give your children wings.
3. Get your creative juices going. Create a "Brainstorming List" of at least ten possible activities you could try with your children.
4. Give thought to one of these areas: holiday traditions, cheap mini-vacations, bedtime rituals, birthday parties, mealtime enrichment. Develop a plan and carry it out.

Chapter Twelve

GOD IS OUR ONLY CIRCUMSTANCE

You may face circumstances that add particular difficulties to your task as a mother. You may have a child with a disability or a husband who is antagonistic to the things of Christ. You may have the additional pressure of holding down a job or the adjustment of a new baby arriving after your other children are grown. Perhaps you are carrying the parenting load alone, without the support of a husband. Or maybe motherhood just isn't what you expected.

Lila Trotman, widow of the founder of The Navigators, once said to my husband, "Roger, always remember that God is your only circumstance." God towers above our circumstances. He wants to use the difficult aspects of our lives for our good. "In all things God works for the good of those who love him, who have been called according to his purpose" (Romans 8:28).

Whether the difficult circumstances we face are from God's hand or because of our own poor choices, He is able to produce from them something positive and glorifying to Himself.

179

The apostle Paul had problems—physical illness, beatings, imprisonments, stonings, hunger, and more (2 Corinthians 11:23-28). But whatever the circumstance, Paul strove to know Christ and to make Him known.

God did not allow these circumstances in order to frustrate Paul's desire to experience Christ more fully, or to stifle the progress of the gospel. Instead, God intended them to form boundaries for Paul's life. Paul did not kick down these boundaries so that he might get on with the job as he saw it. Rather, he accepted the boundaries and worked within them. He sang and praised God from a gloomy prison, used appearances before questioning officials to testify of his faith in Christ, gathered firewood and encouraged others after a shipwreck, and worked with his hands making tents amid a busy missionary schedule.

God has set boundaries around your life, too. Your children form part of the boundaries. But remember, God brings the circumstances to better define your life, not to restrict it.

DONNA'S CIRCUMSTANCES

"Physically speaking, your son may become a vegetable," the doctor informed Donna and her husband. Donna had suspected that her second child's development was abnormally slow, but she wasn't prepared for the doctor's blunt diagnosis. However, she refused to accept the doctor's pronouncement as final. God had created Timothy, so she would do everything she could to unlock his potential.

With this decision, Donna's life took on a new direction. She continually prayed that God would lead her to resources that would educate and encourage her as she committed herself to stimulate Timothy's development.

She read helpful books and studies, wrote letters and telephoned experts and institutions that might help, and took classes dealing with the development of human potential. She gave Timothy countless rubdowns and brushed his skin to stimulate development of his nerve endings. She spent hours teaching him how to crawl, how to hold a spoon, and how to relax enough to breathe normally.

The hours of exhausting labor produced positive results. "When I put out effort, God worked," Donna says now. Friends and doctors who have watched Timothy's progress are amazed. He is active in Scouts and in his church youth group. He rides a bicycle and is at the top of his special education class in reading.

Donna and her husband see an obvious correlation between Timothy's development and their own spiritual growth. Something happened in their own lives when they committed themselves to helping Timothy. God used their commitment to develop greater spiritual maturity in them.

Joan's Circumstances

Joan experienced the emotional trauma of an unwanted divorce. She felt painfully rejected and abandoned. She now carried many responsibilities alone—the children (ages fourteen, eleven, ten, and nine), the home, the yard, the car, the bills, the pets.

"But the hardest thing for me as a mother," Joan says, "was that there was no one to back me up. Before, my husband stepped in if the children showed any disrespect. Now, I must demand it without his support. And it's tough not to have someone else to talk with who knows the children well."

Shortly after the divorce, Joan accepted a job as a

substitute teacher. The hours were short and she wouldn't have to work every day. But as she rushed home after school on the days she did work, did a few necessary jobs around the house, and started dinner, Joan felt at a disadvantage. She hadn't seen her children come in from school, heard their conversation, or gotten an idea of what was happening in their lives.

She discovered her resources were too low to give herself to her children. She wanted to instill clear standards and convictions for her children to make decisions, but because of her fatigue and strain, she sensed she had failed in this important part of her mothering task. Joan found it too easy to say yes to activities that would occupy the children when she would have said no before. She was too weary to stand firm in her convictions.

Anxious and confused, Joan sank down beside her bed and cried out to God: "Lord, how do you want me to handle these new stresses and responsibilities? You know I've felt a deep commitment to be a mother in the home. Did the divorce change everything, or should I stay at home? But how could I? We couldn't survive financially."

God reminded Joan that there had never been a day in the past when He hadn't taken care of her. Joan determined she would remain at home and trust God to supply their needs. And He has.

One windy December night, Joan's children heard a mysterious knock at the door. The children, as they had been taught, asked, "Who's there?"

No one answered. The frightened children called Joan. Cautiously, she cracked the door—and found a Christmas tree on their front porch. Her son yelled into the night, "Please come back. We want to thank you."

God has provided through gifts from friends and

from their church, money from a forgotten savings account and from baby-sitting jobs, and more dramatic provisions. Joan's daughter had an opportunity to be involved in a Christian training program in another city, but the $200 airfare seemed out of sight. Joan prayed, "Lord, You could wave Your hand over those airline computers and do something for us." Later that day an airlines agent phoned. Excitedly, he told Joan he had found a round-trip ticket for $116. "It can't be right," he exclaimed, "but it must be. It was on the computer."

Joan believes her decision to remain at home has given stability to the family in a time of instability and trauma. Being there has given Joan more opportunities to give direction, to guide her children in thinking through the issues facing them, and to help them avoid unwise decisions.

In her own pain and trauma, Joan sees the good hand of God on her life. Like a husband—"For your Maker is your husband—the Lord Almighty is his name" (Isaiah 54:5)—God meets her emotional needs, and provides for and gives direction to her family. His goodness and love expressed to Joan and her children intensifies her confidence in Him.

Her children gain as they see God's ability to meet every kind of need: a Christmas tree, money for the dentist, healing for the family dog. Joan's children have experienced firsthand the compassion and faithfulness of God—their only circumstance.

LENA'S CIRCUMSTANCES

Now a grandmother, Lena recalls years ago sitting on her mother's porch and complaining, "I have too many kids." She mentioned the near impossibility of having her own regular devotional time or memorizing Scripture with nine children underfoot.

Lena had a fervent desire to put God first in her life. And despite the busyness of raising nine children, she was succeeding more and more frequently in wringing time from her hectic schedule for her personal spiritual development. But this had been one of those unsuccessful days.

Lena's mother spoke softly and sympathetically. "Guess the Lord made a mistake when He gave you nine children. Maybe He'll take some of them away from you; then you won't have so many."

Lena was appalled at such a thought—but also sobered. One by one her children's faces passed before her. She loved them all. God had given her more than enough love to embrace them all, and she knew He could also give her enough strength, wisdom, and patience.

When Lena felt overwhelmed by the demands of her growing family, she often returned to her mother's porch. The older woman would rock slowly and remind Lena of a story about two women: The first woman, a mother with small children, envied the second woman's spotless windows. But the second woman, who was childless after years of marriage, insisted that her neighbor's windows were beautiful with their smudges and fingerprints.

Lena's mother also reminded her to thank and praise God for her children. This act of the will reflects an acknowledgment that God is our only circumstance.

MARY'S CIRCUMSTANCES

Mary had six-year-old and seven-year-old daughters when her husband died during the Great Depression. She wanted to influence her daughters for the Lord and didn't want anyone else to bring them up. So she turned their home into a boarding house for Harvard University students, and also maintained a chiropractic practice there.

Mary taught her daughters to look to their heavenly Father to meet their needs as they would have looked to their earthly father if he had lived. She read the Bible with them and encouraged them to look for answers there. Despite tight finances, Mary sent her girls to Christian camps where they might be stimulated in their walk with Christ. She invited missionaries and others with a warm heart for God's work into their home.

But most of all, Mary herself trusted God. The two daughters grew up with memories of a godly mother who invited the poor and lonely to their home to eat, who shared Christ with others throughout her life, who loved God's Word, and who experienced the stabilizing presence of Christ in daily life.

Mary knew God was her only circumstance.

YOUR CIRCUMSTANCES

In this chapter you met mothers who faced difficult circumstances with God's help. They allowed the environment in which God placed them to become a positive factor in their growth and their children's growth as well. The specific limitations or hardships they faced became steppingstones to new depths with God.

You may be facing a particularly difficult set of circumstances. But the same God who gave these women comfort, strength, encouragement, and wisdom stands waiting to give them also to you: "He tends his flock like a shepherd: He gathers the lambs in his arms and carries them close to his heart; he gently leads those that have young" (Isaiah 40:11).

God promises to lead us, though the way He leads you may be entirely different from how He led Donna, Joan, Lena, or Mary. But we should all pray, read God's Word, seek counsel, wait on God's peace in our hearts, and act in faith.

Let us ponder the greatness of the God we serve and know assuredly that He is our only circumstance.

QUESTIONS FOR REFLECTION OR DISCUSSION

1. What boundaries or special circumstances has God allowed to define your life?
2. In what ways do these boundaries become opportunities for growth?
3. What do you most need from God in your particular circumstance?
4. List three things to ask God for today.

Chapter Thirteen

PARENTING BY FAITH OR FEAR?

◆ Does the state of the world ever make you wish you could gather your family together and run to the hills?

◆ Does rearing godly children in this society seem an impossible challenge?

◆ Do you see negative things in your children's lives that scare you to death?

As a young woman in the sixties I heard Christian women discussing whether they would bring children into such a vile and uncertain world. Kruchev had hammered his shoe on the table at a United Nations meeting and said that the USSR would bury the U.S. We have seen tremendous upheaval since then. Circumstances change. Today our "atheistic enemy" is now one of the most fertile mission fields in the world, more responsive to the gospel than our own country.

I suppose every generation has reasons to fear bringing up children. This world is a hostile environment, no doubt about it. But I wonder if we, like those women in the sixties, don't often worry needlessly over things that will never become reality.

A few years ago I met a mother with her infant—her firstborn—in her arms, who said, "I love being a mother, but I'm so afraid of her teenage years." Perhaps our fears about the teenage years precipitate some of the problems. Undoubtedly, when we fear what may happen in the future, we rob today of strength and joy.

Fear often originates and multiplies in our minds, in our imaginations. I've known this fear, perhaps you have too. Of course, we're not the first to worry over threats that never materialized. In the Old Testament a king receives word that his enemies have formed an alliance. The news intimidates and "the hearts of Ahaz and his people were shaken, as the trees of the forest are shaken by the wind." Quaking, trembling, quivering fear. Panic spreads—and nothing had happened. God sends word to Ahaz, "Be careful, keep calm and don't be afraid. Do not lose heart because of [them]" (Isaiah 7:2,4).

After God acknowledges the threat to King Ahaz, "the Sovereign Lord says: 'It will not take place, it will not happen'" (verse 7). Then, God warns him: "If you do not *stand* firm in your faith, you will not *stand* at all" (verse 9, emphasis added).

In Hebrew whenever God repeats the same word in a sentence it is a signal to take careful note. He is making the strongest kind of statement, issuing the most forceful kind of warning.

What are the evidences that we are standing firm in our faith? We are to be careful, keep calm, not be afraid, and not lose heart. We must focus our eyes on God, not on the armies amassing on our borders, not on the coming teenage years.

FEAR NOT, FEAR GOD

God never tells us to be afraid. He tells us to hate evil, flee evil, and to be alert and wise about evil, but not to fear evil. God does not tell us to fear the times. In fact, He commands us not to be alarmed (Matthew 24:6). God sometimes stirs fear in our enemies to accomplish His purposes, but He does not give the spirit of fear to His people (2 Timothy 1:7).

Throughout Scripture God both chides and comforts His people with the phrase "Fear not" or "Do not be afraid." From the first "Fear not" recorded in the Bible in Genesis to the last in Revelation, God unites those words to some statement about Himself. In Genesis He tells Abram, "Do not be afraid, Abram. I am your shield, your very great reward" (Genesis 15:1). In the last book of the Bible God speaks to the apostle John, "Do not be afraid. I am the First and the Last. I am the Living One; I was dead, and behold I am alive for ever and ever! And I hold the keys of death and Hades" (Revelation 1:17-18). When God says, "Do not be afraid," He means to lift our eyes off the circumstance and focus our gaze on Him.

"Fear not" were the very words the angel spoke to Mary, our Lord's mother (Luke 1:30), and He has been speaking those same words to mothers ever since. He knows our tendency to succumb to fear and the debilitating results on us and our children. He does not say that dangers don't exist. They do. Sometimes our worst fears do come upon us. Even then, it is who God is, what God says, and that God is with us that really matters.

We are, unfortunately, given to fearing the wrong things and the wrong people. God tells us to fear Him. This phrase is frequently repeated in the Bible. Fearing

189

God means we are to take God seriously, to regard Him as holy, to worship, trust, and obey Him.

I used to cling to Psalm 34:7 in my times of terror: "The angel of the Lord encamps around those who fear him, and he delivers them." But the promise for deliverance is not for those who are afraid, but for those who fear the Lord.

What Does This Mean for Us As Mothers?

Fear Does More Harm Than Good

Recognize that your fears do your family more harm than good. Fears make us controlling. Fears make us tense. Fears show us, at that moment, not to be people of faith. Fears show us, at that moment, not to be people of hope. And unfortunately, fears often show us, at that moment, not to be people of love. Just as love casts out fear (1 John 4:18), it seems fears cast out love. Parents often drive their children from them and from faith by their fears.

Our fears may press us either to frenzied decision or paralyzed indecision, to rash and regrettable words or a petrified silence, to unwarranted suspicions or unwise denial. For certain, our fears do our families more harm than good.

God Is in Control

Acknowledge that God has chosen you and your family to live exactly where you are at exactly this time in history. If we charted history on a graph to determine the best time to rear children, we would be hard-pressed to find a good time. After Adam and Eve sinned it was all downhill. In fact, if we were drawing our graph I believe we would have a hard time deciding whether times were good times or bad times. Would we want to rear children during the golden age of the Old Testament, when David was king? Adultery, rape, and murder were part of the royal family's story. Would the years when Jesus walked this earth be a good time? No other period was graced with the physical presence of God come in flesh, but hundreds of babies were slaughtered in Bethlehem within two years of His birth (Matthew 2:13-18). The land where Jesus was born was under enemy occupation, the religious establishment was cold and corrupt, and God had been silent for roughly 400 years prior to His coming. Was the first century of Christianity a good time or a bad time? The church was afire, the good news was spreading, but believers were being torn apart by lions.

Are we in a good time or a bad time? Obviously, we see many grievous things in our culture. But, perhaps more mothers gather to pray for their children and their schools today than any other time in history. Around the United States high school students meet at the flagpole before class to pray. Whenever God moves His people to gather together to pray, He hears and does something extraordinary.

But suppose this really is one of the worst times. God assures us that He has chosen us to live at this specific time of history for a purpose: "From one man he made every nation of men, that they should inhabit the whole earth; and he determined the times set for them and the exact places where they should live. God did this so that men would seek him and perhaps reach out for him and find him, though he is not far from each one of us" (Acts 17:26-27).

The parable of the weeds provides us with a helpful

191

picture of life on earth (Matthew 13:24-30,36-43). The servants of the landowner are distressed because an enemy has sown weeds among the good seed. The landowner tells his servants to wait until harvest to separate the two crops. For us as well, the bad and the good must grow up together.

God Calls Us to Faith, Hope, and Love

"Now faith is being sure of what we hope for and certain of what we do not see" (Hebrews 11:1). Faith and hope are intertwined. Both are tied to believing that what God says is true. Both have to do with unseen realities. Faith says, "I believe what God says about the invisible." Hope says, "I believe what God says about the future."

In heaven we will have no need for faith or hope; all will be visible, tangible reality. But love has a place for eternity. Perhaps this is why it is said: "And now these three remain: faith, hope and love. But the greatest of these is love" (1 Corinthians 13:13).

As mothers, we exercise our faith when we look beyond what is visible. Although Saint Augustine (354–430) had a believing, praying mother, he was involved in immoral living and dabbled in strange philosophies and sects. Augustine was thirty before he became a follower of Christ. William Wilberforce (1759–1833) grew up in a home where Christ was honored, but was absorbed in the sporting and social life. Wilberforce came to true faith through a tutor at Queens College where the two of them read aloud to each other literary classics and the Bible and discussed what they read. After his conversion to Christ, Wilberforce was discipled by John Newton, the converted former slave ship captain who wrote the great hymn "Amazing Grace." Newton encouraged Wilberforce to memorize Scripture, do Bible study, and be Christ's man in the British Parliament where Wilberforce spent most of his public life passing legislation against slavery.

My point? Just because your children are not where you would like to see them at this point in time does not mean all hope is lost. Keep praying and trusting God to work. Pray specifically for the people that God might bring into their lives to influence them. We have all heard dramatic stories of conversion where God touched people who did not have the privilege of learning of Christ in their homes. Our hearts beat faster as we hear their stories. We exalt in the fact that God can reach down and redeem in amazing ways. But often when it comes to our own children we need the challenge to faith: if God can create something from nothing as He did in creation and if He can make something good from something bad, certainly He can yet touch your child as He touched Augustine and Wilberforce.

Encourage Others
God wants us to encourage each other to faith.

"Is there any particular need I should address?" I asked the woman who arranged for me to speak to the women at her church. "Goodness! They're scaring each other to death," she said. "They're convinced its impossible to raise good kids today."

It dishonors God when we feed one another's fears, instead of encouraging each other to trust God and to take heart. God calls us to stir each other to faith and good works especially in these difficult times (Hebrews 10:24-25).

Fear may be one of the Enemy's most powerful strategies. Fear has a way of taking over, of causing us to doubt God, of pushing aside good judgment, of grabbing us by the throat and bullying us into a corner. Neither Jesus nor Paul sidestepped the reality of evil. They painted evil in dark terms, but they never suggested that the state of the world should paralyze believers with fear, nor that we should feed one another's fears. If we fear evil instead of fearing God, evil has power over us.

God has given many promises that He is stronger than evil and that He will be with us and help us. Satan is part of God's creation, inferior to God in every way and in every degree, limited by God in scope and power. The apostle John reminds us: "You, dear children, are from God and have overcome them, because the one who is in you is greater than the one in the world" (1 John 4:4).

It dishonors God when we talk as if the end were still up for grabs, as if we weren't sure who would win the battle between good and evil. The end is written: Jesus is victor.

God is honored when those who fear God, not evil, talk with each other. "Then those who feared the Lord talked with each other, and the Lord listened and heard. A scroll of remembrance was written in his presence concerning those who feared the Lord and honored his name" (Malachi 3:16). I see the Lord looking down on a scene that delights Him. Those who take Him seriously are talking with each other about His faithfulness, His promises, His tender mercies and loving kindness. They may be enjoying tea together or suffering in a dreary dungeon; they may be mothers rejoicing over the robust spiritual health of their children or looking to God in faith for wayward children. The situation is immaterial. The spirit and content of the meeting is everything: God is taken seriously.

The scene is so pleasing to God that He calls in

heavenly scribes to record the conversation, to capture permanently this high point in the history of humanity. For after all, in God's eyes aren't the high points of history those times when His people count on His character and His Word?

God Calls Us to Live with the Tensions of Faith

To live by faith is to live with tensions, with blurred lines and with an uncomfortable lack of definition, because God wants us to look to Him for wisdom, strength, and direction as we parent our children and live our lives. Although God gives some precise negative commands: do not lie, do not commit adultery, the body of His communication to us is presented in round, general terms. For example, God tells us to love Him with all our heart, mind, and strength; to honor our parents, to love others as ourselves. The latter injunctions are clear, but the way of applying them is not specified. The application of "do not lie" is plain, but the application of "love others as yourself" is not. Loving others might be applied by taking a needy family a casserole, not speaking while someone else is talking, rescuing a drowning child, or a million other possibilities. When we mother by faith, trusting God and seeking to implement what He asks of us, the out-working will, and should, vary from family to family, from situation to situation.

God will lead you into individualized applications tailor-made for your family. For example, should you give your child a public school, Christian school, or home school education? God bids each family to pray and seek His counsel. No one answer is right for everyone. God may in fact lead a family to use many different schooling options. The schooling issue illustrates a multitude of other areas where we may learn from God and exercise faith as we make decisions in our families.

There is no one answer to how we handle the television, music, computer, or dating. Each family must come to their conclusions before God in faith.

As we endeavor to follow God, fear often intrudes to test our faith. Fears come in many forms. We worry that God might not lead us or that we might not be able to distinguish His promptings. We worry about outside forces: the media, popular culture, and peer pressure.

Of course, peer pressure can cause problems. Unfortunately, when the phrase *peer pressure* is mentioned mothers usually think solely of the destructive squeeze our children feel to conform. But mothers succumb, too. Sometimes the peer pressure of other Christian mothers wrongly dictates our actions and defines our anxieties. Instead of looking to the Lord for direction, we look around us for cues and approval.

The result is often a rigid picture of what a life following Jesus should look like. We fix upon a single picture: how kids should dress or wear their hair; whether the godly should choose Christian school, public school, or home school for their children. We must neither yield to peer pressure ourselves, nor judge parents who seek to follow the Lord but decide directions different from ours.

We need each other; we are a body. We need to challenge and encourage one another, to learn from one another. The danger comes when one specific application is held up as the only right course of action.

The Struggle to Live Relevantly in This World
If God allowed us to retreat from this world, huddled together in delightful commune with others of like mind, we would be released from some of the stresses that accompany the life of those who take His call seriously. But

196

God calls His people to make Him known. This requires involvement in this world and brings with it complexities and tensions. The difficulty comes in trying to balance the desire to protect our children and the realization that if they can't relate to people there is little hope of reaching them for Christ. The questions are obvious and difficult. For example: Should I allow my children to watch television? If so, what programs? How will I counter the negative impact? What real food for the mind and soul will I feed them?

Once into these complex issues I must realize that my conclusions before God may be different from some other parents who are also seeking God's direction. God has peculiar plans for each family, each child. It only follows that we won't all look the same.

❖　　❖　　❖

Don't run to the hills to escape the evil of this world. Raising godly children right where you are is possible. Ask God to work in your children's lives. Take heart. Be calm. Be careful. Don't be afraid. Trust God.

QUESTIONS FOR REFLECTION OR DISCUSSION

1. Name three things you worried about that never happened.
2. Write "be careful, keep calm, don't be afraid, don't lose heart" on a card to remind you to trust God and not give way to fear. Describe how each of the above phrases (i.e., "be careful") can help you parent by faith instead of fear.
3. How do your fears negatively affect your parenting?
4. What ideas from the chapter are most helpful to you?

AUTHOR

JEAN FLEMING and her husband, Roger, live in Colorado Springs. They have three grown children and two grandchildren. Roger and Jean are on staff with The Navigators and have served in California, Korea, Okinawa, Arizona, and Washington.

Jean is the author of *Finding Focus in a Whirlwind World* (Roper) and *The Homesick Heart* (NavPress). In addition to her writing ministry, Jean speaks to women's groups.

Draw closer to God.

The Homesick Heart

We all have yearnings we can't articulate.
This book will show you how your longings actually
reflect God's own longing for you in order to bring
you into closer communion with Him.

The Homesick Heart
(Jean Fleming) $8

When the Soul Listens

Learn to listen to God and interact with Him
through prayer. Discover spiritual direction
through contemplative living that will lead
you to find rest and guidance in God.

When the Soul Listens
(Jan Johnson) $10

Get your copies today at your local bookstore, or call
(800) 366-7788 and ask for offer **#2111.**

If you liked A MOTHER'S HEART, be sure to check out these other resources designed just for mothers.

Mothers Have Angel Wings

This special collection of stories about motherhood
will inspire, encourage, and challenge you as it explores specific
biblical truths and how they relate to being a mom.
Mothers Have Angel Wings
(Carol Kent) $12

A Mother's Legacy

Women of the Bible struggled with motherhood in much the
same way mothers do today. Learn from ten biblical women
whose struggles and victories are as real
today as they were centuries ago.
A Mother's Legacy
(Jeanne Hendricks) $7

Train Up a Mom

Filled with real-life stories, encouragement, and tips
for becoming a godly mother, *Train Up a Mom* uses
Bible study to teach mothers the importance of training
themselves in godliness in order to raise godly children.
Train Up a Mom
(Vollie Sanders) $7

Get your copies today at your local bookstore, or call
(800) 366-7788 and ask for offer **#2111.**

NAVPRESS
BRINGING TRUTH TO LIFE
www.navpress.com

Prices subject to change without notice.